J██
Hall
Pilgrim neighbors

CAPE ANN
Gloucester

Massachusetts

Plymouth
Bay
Plymouth

Buzzard
Aptucxe
(Bourne)

Ocean

Nantucket Sound

Pilgrim Neighbors

MORE TRUE PILGRIM STORIES

PILGRIM NEIGHBORS: *More True Pilgrim Stories* was prepared in cooperation with, and approved by, Plimoth Plantation in Plymouth, Massachusetts.

Pilgrim Neighbors

MORE TRUE PILGRIM STORIES

by Elvajean Hall

illustrated by Jon Nielsen

RAND McNALLY & COMPANY

CHICAGO • NEW YORK • SAN FRANCISCO

For *Massasoit,*
Wamsutta, and
Iyanough—three "Pilgrim Neighbors"
whom I should like to have known.

J
973.2

CONTENTS

FOREWORD

WE ARE ALL familiar with some stories of the Pilgrims
—the flight from Scrooby to Holland, the fateful deci-
sion after nearly twelve years to go to the New World,
the adventures on the *Mayflower* at sea, the birth of
the babies Oceanus Hopkins and Peregrine White,
and the story of the first "Thanksgiving." At this point
most children's books about the Pilgrims come to an
end.

Few know of the conflict that existed almost from
the start in Plymouth, for the Pilgrims were not a
close-knit group. Among them were Separatists and
"middle-of-the-road" Puritans, a sprinkling of Church
of England members, as well as a few who probably
professed no religion at all but saw in the *Mayflower* a
chance to get passage to the New World. Even the
colony's "backers" in England held many different
views; the only thing they were agreed on was a desire to make money.

The story of the Pilgrims really had just begun at
the time Massasoit and about ninety of his people

dropped in on Plymouth for the historic three-day visit of feasting and games some time in the early autumn of 1621—a celebration that has come to be known as the first "Thanksgiving."

During their first year in the New World, the Pilgrims' only neighbors were Indians. Small groups gradually began to arrive from England. Some proved good neighbors; others so bad they threatened the safety of all. It was 1628 before the Pilgrims had more than a handful of neighbors other than Indians.

All the stories in *Pilgrim Neighbors* take place between 1621 and 1691—and all are true.

Many customs of the New England Indians seemed strange to Englishmen when first they arrived. For this reason, several passages have been worked into the text of *Pilgrim Neighbors* that were taken directly from reports and letters written during the first few years in America. They tell in the Pilgrims' own words what life was like in the colony.

Sometimes only a sentence or phrase has been quoted from an original source; at other times material has been paraphrased or greatly telescoped.

Edward Winslow described Indian customs in great detail in the manuscript that he carried to England in 1623. He frankly confessed in this manuscript that many of the Pilgrims' first impressions had been incorrect. Now that he had known their Indian neighbors for two years, Winslow felt in a better position to write accurately of their customs and beliefs.

One of the strangest Indian customs was the practice of changing names. Many Indians shed their childhood names when they reached manhood and took one they considered more suited to their personality. Massasoit went under several names.

An important character in *Pilgrim Neighbors* is Hobomok, Massasoit's trusted adviser and representative to the Pilgrims. Hobomok's name meant "Devil" in the Wampanoag language. He probably chose this name himself when he reached a high position in the tribe.

Hobomok is spelled in many different ways, as most Indian names of people and places are. Pilgrims were not as fussy about spelling as people are today, and every writer in early New England seemed to spell as the words sounded to his ear! The settlers spelled even their own names in several different ways on early documents, and often the form they liked best is not at all the spelling their descendants now use.

In the early 1620's, many colonists had a standard of living not much higher than that of neighboring Indians. However, as time went on, the life of the settlers improved so that many of them were living as well as they would have lived in England. Every year the gulf widened between colonists and Indians who were trying desperately to hold to the ways of their ancestors in a changing and shrinking world.

King Philip's War was a tragic struggle between the new and the old in New England.

E. H.

Chapter 1

GETTING ACQUAINTED

THE TWENTY-NINTH of September, 1621, was a beautiful day. A warm, lazy Indian-summer haze hung over the shore as a large open sail-boat, or shallop as it was then called, worked its way into Boston harbor. In the boat were thirteen men: ten Pilgrims, Squanto, and two other Indian guides. They had come up the coast from Plymouth, a distance of forty-four miles.

Short, stocky Myles Standish, the Pilgrims' red-headed military leader, was in command. The party had come to explore the land around Massachusetts Bay. They hoped to meet their Indian neighbors to the north and trade with them.

The men were tired. They had left Plymouth the night before, expecting to reach their destination the next morning. But the wind had been light and the distance much greater than they had expected, and so it was late in the afternoon before they anchored off an island they named "Trevore" in honor of the English sailor in their group. Today it is called Thompson's Island.

They saw no sign of life. No dogs ran to the beach and barked and snapped at their approach, no squaws or children were gathering firewood or digging for clams. There was not even the smoke of a distant campfire. When night came, they slept in the shallop.

The next morning Standish began to explore in earnest. After crossing the narrow channel that separated the island from a rocky headland, the men leaped ashore at the foot of a cliff on the mainland. Here they breakfasted on lobsters they found mysteriously lying on the rocks.

"I wish I knew whose lobsters we are eating, for they must belong to somebody; lobsters do not jump onto a neat pile on the beach by themselves!" said Standish with a worried laugh.

After breakfast, Standish appointed guards to watch the shallop, while he took several men with him to search for the Indians he was sure must be living nearby. They had not gone far when they met an old Indian woman on her way to pick up the lobsters that the Indians had left on the rocks an hour before. Standish confessed that they had eaten all of them, and paid her for their breakfast with some of the articles they had brought for trade.

The squaw told Squanto, who was acting as interpreter, that the name of her chief, or sachem, was Obbatinewat. "He lives in great fear of the terrible squaw-sachem of the Massachusetts and the warlike Tarrantines still farther to the north," she confided. "So great is his fear that he dares not camp long in any one place, and is always on the move." Deciding that the Pilgrim explorers meant them no harm, the woman agreed to take them to Obbatinewat.

After he had exchanged promises of friendship with the Pilgrims, Obbatinewat reluctantly agreed to lead Standish to the much-feared squaw-sachem of the Massachusetts, the widow of Nanepashemet. "I think I know about where she lives," he said. "I have been told it is near the banks of the Mystic River."

As the Pilgrims headed toward the Mystic River, they marveled at the size of the bay and the beauty of the wooded islands that dotted its surface. Here and there they saw the ruins of deserted Indian farms, just as they had seen them around Plymouth. It looked as if the same sickness must have wiped out the Massachusetts Bay Indians that had killed the Indians to the south of them.

Night had fallen by the time the party reached the mouth of the Mystic, and Standish felt it was too late to go farther. They camped a second night on board.

The next morning they again went ashore, and Standish again left some of the men behind to guard the boat. This time the party pushed inland.

Three miles along the trail they came to a deserted village. After another mile they reached the spot where Nanepashemet had lived. The dead chief's old wigwam was still standing high on the top of a hill. He had built it about six feet off the ground on a scaffolding of weather-beaten planks supported on poles.

In the swamp, a short distance from the sachem's hut, was his stronghold, a circle about forty or fifty feet across, enclosed by a stake fence. The only entrance to this enclosure was by means of a bridge over two ditches. In the center of the enclosure was the building in which Nanepashemet had been buried.

After they had plodded still another mile through the warm autumn sunshine, the Pilgrims came to a second hilltop stronghold where the Indians told them Nanepashemet had been surprised and murdered by the savage Tarrantines about two years earlier. No one had lived in the dead chief's stockade since his death.

"How much this reminds me of our first days at Plymouth," Standish confided to one of his companions. "Where do you suppose everyone has gone?"

The Pilgrims did not know it, but the news of their approach was traveling ahead of them. In several places they had seen the poles of houses that had been hastily torn down, and once they even had spied a pile of Indian corn hidden under a mat. But they didn't connect these sights with their own arrival.

"Let's rest a few moments," panted Myles Standish as he sent two of the guides ahead to scour the countryside for the missing Indians.

The guides did find some Indian women tugging at the baskets of corn they were dragging away from a village. At first the squaws were terrified, fearing the English would be as fierce as their tribe's enemy, the Tarrantines. When they found that the Pilgrims meant no harm, the squaws agreed to cook them a supper.

"Are there only women here?" puzzled Myles Standish had Squanto ask them. "Have you no men?"

Finally, one Indian man did appear, shaking and trembling with fear. When he was convinced that the Pilgrims had come to trade as they said, and not to plunder, he promised them his furs, and all the furs of his friends.

There was still no sight of the squaw-sachem, Nanepashemet's widow. No matter how much the Pilgrims coaxed and begged the Indians of her tribe, they got the same answer over and over, "She is very far from here." Her loyal people were taking no chances, for they remembered how Nanepashemet had been murdered.

Night was coming on and the Pilgrims prepared to return to their shallop. Squanto looked with greedy eyes at the furs their Indian cooks were wearing. "Let's take the furs from them," he suggested to Standish. "These are a bad people, and they have often threatened you."

Standish brushed him aside saying, "Squanto, you can't steal women's jackets! That is not the way honorable men act."

This did not stop Squanto. He wanted those furs and he meant to have them. His snapping black eyes seemed to say, "If I cannot snatch

"Let's take the furs from them," Squanto suggested

their beaver jackets, I'll get them some other way. I must think fast of a way our captain will allow."

Trotting along beside the squaws, he wheedled and coaxed in the Indian language. Whatever he offered must have pleased them, for suddenly they stopped and sold the furs off their backs. When they realized what they had done, they were embarrassed and wrapped tree branches about their bodies.

That evening the shallop sailed for home with thirteen weary men and the heap of things they had traded. As beautiful Massachusetts Bay faded into the distance, more than one of the Pilgrims thought, *Why couldn't the* "Mayflower" *have brought us here first?*

Chapter 2

SEIZED BY PIRATES

A WEEK OR TWO after the exploring party returned from Massachusetts Bay, the Pilgrims had a surprise visit from Massasoit and ninety of his people. The harvest was in, the weather was warm, and Pilgrims and Indians spent three days feasting, playing games, and giving thanks.

The Pilgrims had hardly recovered from this first Thanksgiving before there was again excitement in Plymouth. A ship, the tiny *Fortune* out of London, suddenly appeared. At first the Pilgrims feared it was an enemy ship, come to rob them.

"If it is, we shall be ready for them!" roared Myles Standish as he took aim with a cannon. "See that every man and boy is armed with a gun or a sword or knife."

The *Fortune* was only one-third the size of the *Mayflower*, but she carried thirty-five passengers. Twelve were friends from Leyden. The rest were "Strangers," a name given by the Leyden Pilgrims to the people in the *Mayflower* whom they had not known before.

But whether the new settlers were relatives, friends, or complete strangers, they all brought welcome news from home. It was exactly a year since the *Mayflower* had first sighted Cape Cod, which meant fourteen long months without any word from those left behind.

Thomas Weston, the London merchant who had helped the *Mayflower* Pilgrims get to the New World, had sent, with the thirty-five new recruits, a cruel and heartless letter to the Pilgrims' governor. He demanded that they pay off, at once, part of their debt to him and berated them because the *Mayflower* had not carried a cargo on her return. It made no difference to him that half of those who came in the *Mayflower* had died during that first dreadful winter.

The *Mayflower* Pilgrims were stunned by

Weston's harsh words. They worked desperately during the two weeks the *Fortune* lingered in Plymouth to fill the ship's hold with clapboard which would bring a very high price in London. They also crammed two hogsheads with beaver and otter skins, which they had traded from the Indians, and put them on board.

The *Fortune* grew smaller and smaller as she left Plymouth Bay. Finally she was no more than a speck on the horizon. Governor William Bradford turned to his oldest friend, Elder Brewster, with a sigh of relief. "If we can get another load off like that one, we shall be free of debt."

He and the other Pilgrims could not guess the terrible fate that would befall the ship as she approached the coast of England.

The little *Fortune* bounced over the waves until she was close to the English coast. It had been a good crossing, as winter crossings go. Then suddenly on January 29, 1622 a great pirate ship swooped down on her. The captain of the pirate ship was in league with the Marquis de Cera, who made his headquarters on an island off the coast of Poitou.

The Marquis held the captain of the *Fortune* prisoner for seven days in his castle. The rest of the company he left to the mercy of his soldiers.

"Take from them anything you like," the crafty Marquis told his men. "A poor and ragged lot these English look, but maybe you will find that they have more than meets the eye."

With this command, the French gladly set to work. They stripped the crew and passengers of what little they had. The soldiers even stole their clothing and the shoes from their feet. They gathered up their captives' possessions, leaving them not even a kettle in which to boil food, or a bowl from which to drink.

While his men were busy looting the passengers and crew, the Marquis claimed for himself the ship's cargo—all the Pilgrims' precious clapboard and the barrels of beaver and otter skins. When these had been taken ashore, the Marquis had the ship stripped of anchor ropes, anchor chain, the two cannon, and the eight

The captain of the "Fortune" struggles as he is brought aboard the French pirate ship

hand guns with ammunition, powder, and shot. He even took their English flag.

Next he seized the letters and opened them. "Here, you read this," the Marquis ordered one of his men as he handed him a letter. "You are the only one here who knows their miserable language."

The Frenchman then read, in halting English, bits from Edward Winslow's letters:

 . . . For the temper of the air here, it agreeth well with that in England and if there be any difference at all, this is somewhat hotter in summer. Some think it to be colder in winter, but I cannot out of experience so say. The air is very clear and not foggy as hath been reported. I never in my life remember a pleasanter year than we have here enjoyed and if we only had cattle, horses and sheep, I think there is no question but men might live here as happily as in any part of the world.

 For fish and fowl, we have great abundance. Our Bay is full of lobsters all summer and affordeth variety of other fish. In September we can take a hogshead of eels in a night with small labor and can dig them out of their beds. All winter we have mussels and clams at our door. Oysters we have none near but we can have them brought by the Indians when we will.

The Marquis rocked with laughter as his man translated the English words into French. "So they have great abundance, do they? Hah, hah, hah! Read me some more."

The officer continued.

In springtime the earth sendeth forth naturally very good salad greens. Here are grapes white and red, strawberries, gooseberries, raspberries, etc.; plums of three sorts: white, black, and red, being almost as good as a damson; abundance of roses: red, white, and damask, single but very sweet indeed. The country wanteth only industrious men to cultivate it.

"Rot," the marquis snorted, as the offcer again paused to translate.

Now because I expect your coming unto us with others of our friends, whose company we much desire, I have thought good to advertise you of a few things needful.

Be careful to have on board your ship a very good bread-room, to put your biscuits in. Let your case for beer and water be iron-bound, for the first tier if not more. Let your meal be so hard trodden in your cask that you shall need an adze or hatchet to work it out with. Trust not too much on us for corn at this time;

for, by reason of the 35 on the *Fortune* who brought nothing we shall have little enough till harvest.

Be sure you can get at some of your meal to eat on the way over. It will much refresh you. Build your cabins on the ship as open as you can and bring good store of clothes and bedding with you. Bring every man a musket or fowling piece. Bring juice of lemons.

If you bring anything for comfort in the country, butter, or salad oil, or both, are very good. Our Indian corn, even the coarsest, maketh as pleasant meal as rice; therefore, do not bring rice unless to eat on the way. Bring paper and linseed oil for your windows; and cotton yarn for your lamps. Let your shot be mostly for big fowls, and bring plenty of powder and shot.

I forbear further to write, for the present, hoping to see you by the next return of a ship here. So I take my leave, commending you to the Lord, for a safe conduct unto us:

Resting in him
Your loving friend
E. W.

Plymouth in New England
this 11th of December 1621

"Hm-n—," muttered the Marquis.

"Sir?" his translator paused a moment, waiting for him to make up his mind.

"Oh, let them keep that one," growled the Marquis.

Whenever an English or a Dutch ship came close, the pirate Marquis had all the prisoners on the *Fortune* stowed under the hatches so that they could not be seen or call for help.

Each day the prisoners grew hungrier, for they had been robbed of all their food.

"Here, feast on these lungs, guts, and gizzards if you want to eat," the Marquis's men taunted them.

Thirteen days slowly went by. Finally the Marquis de Cera decided to let the *Fortune* go. But first he made those on board sign a paper saying that all he had taken from them were two hogsheads of fox skins. "If you do not sign," the wily Marquis threatened, "every one of you shall stay here till you rot!"

Captain Barton and all on board the *Fortune* signed.

Then they were given a little meat, a hogshead of poor wine, bread and vinegar and sent shivering on their way to England.

Chapter 3

MESSAGE OF THE SNAKESKIN

"Has anybody seen Squanto?" asked Edward Winslow, sticking his head into the Common House, where Governor Bradford and Myles Standish were working one day soon after the *Fortune* had sailed. "I see an Indian coming up the beach who looks like a messenger."

"Squanto has gone hunting and may not be back until tomorrow," replied Bradford. "Bring your Indian here and maybe the three of us can figure out his message."

Winslow led in an Indian who carried in his hand a bundle of arrows carefully wrapped in the skin of a large black snake. The Indian refused to return the governor's friendly greeting and kept asking over and over for "Tisquantum," as the Indians called Squanto. Throwing his mysterious snakeskin bundle on the floor, the Indian snarled a few words and turned to leave.

Winslow and Standish could make out little of what he had said, but from the look on his face and the tone of his voice, they knew the Indian was threatening them.

Governor Bradford was puzzled, too. He had no idea what the messenger was trying to say, but he knew that he came from Canonicus, sachem of the Narragansetts, the powerful tribe then living in what is now Rhode Island. The Narragansetts had always been enemies of Massasoit and his Wampanoag Nation and so Bradford knew that Canonicus would hate anyone who was a friend of Massasoit.

Bradford wanted, if possible, to have the Indian wait for Squanto to return. "Take him in charge, Standish," the governor ordered. "But be sure you treat him kindly."

The messenger from Canonicus did not want to wait. He looked with horror at short, chunky Myles Standish, whose red hair gleamed in the sun. He trembled, for he had heard terrible tales of this little man with the red hair and beard who had three weapons: a gun and a sword and the deadly "black sickness" that he kept hidden under his hut for the times when he did not want to use his other weapons! The Indian messenger refused to eat when Standish offered him food. Angrily he stalked up and down and insisted on being allowed to return to his people.

"It is wrong to hold a messenger against his will," Bradford said when evening came and Squanto had still not appeared. "I'm afraid there's nothing we can do now but let him go." So the Indian was set free, and he slipped silently away into the night.

The next day Squanto came home. Bradford showed him the snakeskin wrapped around arrows. "What do you suppose this means?"

Squanto's black eyes flashed with sudden anger. "Arrows wrapped in snakeskin say to all, 'Come out and fight.' The sachem of the Narragansett tells you, 'Soon many arrows fly and many English die.'"

"So that was what that Indian was trying to

tell us all day!" Bradford said, with a laugh. "No wonder he was so anxious to be off! I know a good reply to that message."

First, Bradford tossed the Indian arrows into a corner. Then he began to stuff the snakeskin with shot and powder. When he had finished, he handed the wiggling, bulging skin to Squanto.

"Take this thing back to the sachem of the Narragansetts," he told him. "Tell Canonicus that we have done him no harm but we are ready to fight any time he wants to."

Squanto started off joyfully, though it was a cold and windy day and the trails were covered with snow. He was delighted to be carrying Bradford's message, for he hated the Narragansetts. They were the sworn enemy of his people, the Wampanoag, and had been for as many moons as he could remember. Ever since the dreadful sickness that had wiped out many Wampanoag villages, including Squanto's own, the Narragansett Indians had been powerful. They had not caught the sickness that had killed Massasoit's people.

Squanto carries Bradford's message over the snow-covered trail

When Canonicus saw the snakeskin, he was worried. This was not at all the answer that he had expected.

"The friends of Massasoit send you their thunder and lightning," Squanto announced, trying to place in the chief's own hand the glistening snakeskin now filled with Pilgrim shot and powder.

Canonicus had heard of the deadly weapons that Massasoit's new friends were using. A few of his people had heard them thunder, but none of them had ever touched a gun or seen powder and shot. His warriors crowded round him to gaze at the snake, but no one dared touch it. Canonicus refused to keep it in his village and ordered Squanto to take it back to Plymouth— at once.

"Oh, we have more there," Squanto replied. "We do not need this!" Then he turned on his heel and departed.

Canonicus did not know what to do. He was afraid to keep the snakeskin filled with its deadly "magic." He did not want it in his home. He did not want it in any of his villages, no matter how remote they were. Finally he sent one of his messengers with it to another tribe. They, too, would have nothing to do with the dreaded snakeskin bundle. And so it was sent on from one Indian village to another, bringing terror to all who received it. Finally, after many weeks of traveling from place to place, the snakeskin was returned, unopened, to the Pilgrims.

That was all the people in Plymouth heard of war for some time. But they thought it wise, nevertheless, to protect their settlement, and started work on a stockade that would surround the whole village. This fence was eleven feet high and made of pointed posts driven deep into the ground, then laced together. For a long time watchmen were kept on guard in case of trouble.

Chapter 4

SEND ME SQUANTO'S HEAD
AND HANDS!

SQUANTO AND Hobomok were not friends. Hobomok did not trust Squanto, and Squanto was jealous of Hobomok who was Massasoit's trusted adviser and representative to the Pilgrims.

It was much nicer before there were two Indians here, Squanto often thought to himself. His jealousy grew until it poisoned everything he did. Each time he saw Myles Standish turn to Hobomok, as one warrior to another, Squanto drew closer to Governor Bradford, who seemed to prefer him. Hobomok might suspect what he was up to, but Squanto was very careful to let only his good side show to the Pilgrims.

"I know all the secrets of the white men," Squanto bragged to the Indians around Plymouth. "I even know where they keep the 'black sickness'. . . . They keep it hidden beneath the boards of the floor and can send it at you like a flash out of a cloud in a storm!" Here he would drop his voice to a whisper. "But Squanto has the power to make them change its course . . ." The frightened Indians would then give Squanto presents for protection, and day by day his stories grew and grew.

As spring advanced, the Pilgrims' food ran low. Governor Bradford suggested another trading trip to the Indians living on Massachusetts Bay from whom they had bought corn before.

"Do not go at this time," Hobomok warned. "I see trouble and Squanto has a hand in it. He has been slipping into the woods and meeting secretly with medicine men for some days now. Beware when an Indian acts secretly. If he is doing what he knows is right, he always acts openly."

Bradford talked with Standish, Winslow, and a few others. "We cannot hole ourselves in, for that would show for sure that we are afraid," Standish warned.

The foraging party had no more than started, with Squanto and Hobomok as guides, when a friend of Squanto rushed up to the Plymouth gate, panting and covered with blood. "The Narragansetts and Massachusetts are going to attack Plymouth, and Massasoit plans to join them!" he gasped. "At the risk of my life, I escaped to warn you." All the time he was speaking he kept glancing over his shoulder, as if expecting to see the attackers appear.

Bradford had the shallop called back at once.

"What Squanto's friend told you is not true," said Hobomok angrily. "I am a Pinese, one of the Wampanoag War Council, and I would know at once if an attack is planned."

But Bradford was worried, for the Pilgrims dared not take a chance. "I cannot understand what is going on and why Squanto seems to have a part in it," he said in a puzzled voice. "Why, Squanto is one of our oldest friends! Why should he plot against us?"

However, to be on the safe side, the governor asked Hobomok to send his squaw to Massasoit's home at Sowams, pretending another errand. "If any warlike preparations are going on there, she will be sure to see them."

"All is quiet in Sowams," the squaw reported when she got back.

As soon as the Pilgrims heard this welcome news, Standish and his trading party set out once more in the shallop.

Someone told the story of Squanto's double dealing to Massasoit. He was furiously angry and sent a messenger to Governor Bradford at once, demanding Squanto's life for having falsely accused him of plotting against the Pilgrims.

Governor Bradford did not know what to do. He could not afford to offend Massasoit. Still, he did not want to send Squanto to his death, especially when he remembered the many good things that Squanto had done to help the Pilgrims in the past. It grieved Bradford to have the Indian, whom he had trusted and taken into his own home, prove dishonest. Bradford knew Squanto deserved to be punished, but he did not want to have him put to death.

Turning to Massasoit's messenger, he nodded slowly. "I agree with your great sachem that Squanto deserves to be punished," he said, thinking fast. "It is a great crime for a man to betray either his king or his friends. But I beg that Squanto's life be spared—not for Squanto's sake, but because we need him so badly in Plymouth."

The messenger took this message back to Massasoit, who was not satisfied. A second time he sent runners to Bradford. This time they came bearing gifts. Massasoit reminded Bradford that Squanto was one of his subjects and could not be held by the Pilgrims if he wanted him. Much to Bradford's horror, the messenger offered him many beaver skins if he would consent to Squanto's death.

"It is an Indian custom," the messenger explained, "for a sachem to send his own knife to cut off the head of one of his people. I have brought you Ousamequin's knife that we may cut off Tisquantum's head and hands and bring them to him, as is the custom."

Keeping his voice low and calm, Governor Bradford replied, "But it is not the custom of the English to sell men's lives for a price. I would not do it for all the beaver skins in America!"

Bradford sent for Squanto, who had not tried to run away even though he knew the messenger had come to cut off his head.

Squanto had courage. He walked boldly forward until he stood in front of Hobomok. "You are to blame for all this," he growled. Then he

"I have brought you Ousamequin's knife," the messenger said to Bradford

Squanto walked boldly forward until he stood in front of Hobomok

turned to Bradford, who he felt still was his friend, and said in a quieter tone, "And you are the one who must decide if I am to die. . . ."

Beads of sweat stood out on Bradford's forehead, and his face turned a dreadful, chalky gray. Slowly he began to speak. "I have decided," he began, but got no further.

"A boat! A boat! There is a strange boat beyond yonder head!" screeched John Billington, as he came racing up from the beach to stand panting in front of the governor.

"Just a moment," cried Governor Bradford, grasping at any delay. "I must first see what that boat is before I can turn Squanto over to anybody. . . ."

Impatient and furious because Bradford's stalling had not fooled them, the angry messengers waited hour after hour. Finally they returned to Massasoit without Squanto, his head, or his hands. But from that day until the day of his death, Squanto did not dare leave the protection of the Pilgrims. He knew that if he did, Massasoit would get his head and hands.

Chapter 5

SQUANTO'S LAST TRIP

THE MYSTERIOUS ship, whose arrival saved Squanto's life, turned out to be only a shallop from the *Sparrow* bringing mail and seven men from Maine.

The men had been sent by Thomas Weston, who was still angry that the struggling little colony could not meet his demands. "What I need is a fistful of red-blooded, able-bodied men who aren't always a-praying!" he told a friend. "I'll send out another party and this time they are going to be tough—really tough. There will be no ailing women and whining, sniveling children tagging along."

Weston combed southern England during the winter of 1621–22 for men who would be the opposite of the Pilgrims whom he hated.

He was successful; he found some of the rough-
est men in all England willing to join his expedition.

Before sending over his main party, Weston
decided to send a few ahead to explore and
choose a place to settle. These men left England
aboard the *Sparrow,* bound for the fishing
grounds off the coast of Maine. Weston's plan
was for them to leave the vessel somewhere in
Maine and make their way down the New England coast.

The seven men in this advance group were
reckless devils—swearing, cursing, and bragg-
ing. However, when their little open sailboat
was taken off the *Sparrow* to be made ready,
they started to worry. One suddenly noticed
they had no supplies. Another realized they did
not know where to go. Still others confessed
they were not seafaring men and did not even
know how to handle a boat. The mate of the
Sparrow, always ready for an adventure, felt
sorry for them and offered to pilot their shallop
in order to get them started.

Even though Weston's advance party had claimed, while they were still at home in England, that they were afraid of nothing, they became more fearful every day they spent in the New World. It was too quiet. It was too lonesome. They had never before been away from people and crowded cities. With only the sound of a bird or the distant cry of an animal to break the stillness, the seven lonesome men wanted to push on—on—on—to any place they would find people.

Hungry, without clothing or supplies, they headed for Plymouth and the Pilgrims whom Weston had scorned.

One of the letters brought by the shallop from the *Sparrow* was written to the Pilgrims by a complete stranger. It was a warning from a friendly sea captain, John Huddleston, who had gone to Virginia many times carrying supplies and passengers from England, but who was now fishing in New England waters near the *Sparrow*. He was worried about the safety of the little colony on Plymouth Bay.

He gave them news of a terrible massacre that had taken place only a few months before in Virginia when Indians, led by Opechabcano, uncle of Pocahontas, suddenly rose and slaughtered 347 English settlers. Huddleston warned the Pilgrims to be on guard every minute against a similar fate.

The grateful Pilgrims sent back a letter to the captain thanking him, and Edward Winslow headed for Maine in the Pilgrims' shallop to try to get food from the English ships nearby. It was that or starve. Captain Huddleston again proved a friend in need. He gave all he could spare from his own ship and persuaded other captains fishing there to help the Pilgrims.

Winslow sailed back to Plymouth as fast as he could with his life-saving cargo. Even in the short time he had been away, he could see his friends had weakened. Some were becoming walking skeletons; others were so bloated they looked scarcely human. And yet the despised Pilgrims planned to share what little they had with their seven ungrateful guests.

Governor Bradford knew that if he divided the food that day, some would eat their share at once and then starve. Each morning, therefore, he issued rations so that everyone would have enough to stay alive until crops ripened.

The Pilgrims did not know that their troubles with Weston's men had only begun. Weston's main party—sixty wild, cursing, brawling ruffians—appeared one day in the ships *Charity* and *Swan*. They landed at Plymouth and, to the Pilgrims' dismay, said that Weston expected the Pilgrims to feed them as long as they stayed in Plymouth.

After some weeks the men decided to settle a few miles north of Plymouth at the spot where the Quincy River empties into the bay. They named their settlement Wessagusset. In no time at all the men at Wessagusset colony had eaten all the provisions that Weston had given them. Then they began to beg from the Indians, and to steal from them.

By this time the Pilgrims were almost as hungry as Weston's men. Their crop—the part that had not been stolen by hungry people before it ripened—was smaller than they had expected. They did not know what to do. There was no way for the Pilgrims to get food honorably from the Indians, because they had used up all their trading articles. It looked as if only a miracle would save them from starvation.

Then, one day, almost as if that miracle had taken place, the *Discovery* put into Plymouth. The captain, who was really a part-time pirate, was this time on an honest voyage and had on board a large supply of trinkets, beads, knives, and other things that could be used for buying corn from the Indians. When he saw how desperate the Pilgrim colony was, he raised his price to six or seven times the usual charge for such trading articles. But still the Pilgrims paid what he asked.

Now that they had something to trade, the Pilgrims decided to send the shallop on a long voyage around Cape Cod, buying along the way all the food they could get the Indians to sell. When Weston's men at Wessagusset heard of the trip to Cape Cod, they asked if they could go, too, in their pinnace, the *Swan*.

The first time the two boats set out they were driven back by a storm. The next time they turned back because Myles Standish had suddenly taken sick with a high fever.

Bradford felt they had no time to lose; they should not even wait for Standish to get better. "I'll lead the expedition myself," he announced. Then he turned to Squanto whom he still liked, in spite of all the trouble over his head and hands. "Squanto, would you like to come along as our guide and interpreter?" he asked.

This was the last time Squanto would ever help the Pilgrims. A few weeks later he, too, came down with a raging fever and, in spite of everything Bradford and the Indians on Cape Cod could do, he grew steadily worse. As Squanto lay dying, he begged Governor Bradford to pray for him. "Pray that I may go to the Englishmen's God in Heaven."

Governor Bradford's eyes filled with tears as he knelt by Squanto's pallet.

Governor Bradford's eyes filled with
tears as he knelt by Squanto's pallet

Chapter 6

CHACHEWUNNEA

"OUR SACHEM is near death!" gasped an Indian runner, panting and covered with sweat, who suddenly appeared at the gate to Plymouth one spring day in 1623.

This was sad news for all the Pilgrims, for Massasoit was their friend. Bradford, Winslow, and Elder Brewster drew aside to talk over what they should do. They knew it was the custom among the Indians, when someone lay ill or dying, to visit him, even from as far away as one hundred miles.

Winslow offered to go to Massasoit, with Hobomok as his guide. A English visitor, then in Plymouth, asked to go with them.

Hobomok was so anxious to get started he could scarcely wait for Winslow to prepare medicine and food. "Hurry, hurry! *Chachewun-nea* (He is dying)," he kept repeating over and over.

As they hurried along the trail, they received many different reports. "You are too late; our great leader is already dead," someone called out.

"No, he is not dead yet, but he will be within a few hours," others warned them as they dashed past.

Indians seldom talked to Pilgrims of their joys and sorrows, but Hobomok could no longer hold in his grief. "*Neen womasu sagimus; neen womasu sagimus* (Oh, my Chief, my dear, my loving Chief)," he moaned over and over under his breath. "Many have I known, but never one like thee . . ."

Then he turned suddenly toward Winslow, and the words came pouring from his heart. "You will never see his like again. He was not like others—false, bloody, and cruel. He was kind and loving. He was easily calmed down when he was angry. He was forgiving to his enemies. Oh, what friend will you have among the Indians when he is gone?" Over and over Hobomok moaned these words as the three men hurried on.

By this time two days had passed since they had set out, and the cold March sun was sinking behind a bank of clouds. Shadows grew black and deep in the forest and the wind whistled through the tree tops. As they came within sight of Sowams, they could hear from a distance the wailing of Massasoit's friends. When they reached the sick chief's lodge, they could hardly force their way in, it was so jammed with his friends.

Massasoit lay on his hard plank bed, his eyes closed.

Five or six medicine men, or "Powahs," as the Indians called them, were hard at work. Their half-naked bodies were painted in many colors, and upon their heads were the horns of beasts. Dancing about the stricken chief, they leaped and yelled and waved their arms in the air to frighten the sickness and keep death away.

Within the circle of their panting, sweating bodies were six or seven women frantically rubbing Massasoit's numb arms and legs to try to keep heat in them.

"It would be hard even for a well man to stand this kind of treatment," thought Winslow.

They leaped and yelled and waved their arms

When the Indians became aware of Hobomok and the two Englishmen from Plymouth,
they tried to make way for them to draw nearer
to the bed. "It is the English," someone bent to
tell Massasoit.

"Who has come?" whispered the sachem, too
ill to recognize the face of his friend.

"Winsnow," someone told him, for the Indians could not pronounce the letter "l."

"I want to speak to him," gasped Massasoit
as he put out a feeble hand in welcome.

Winslow seized the hand that groped for his
and bent over the couch.

"*Keen Winsnow* (Are you truly Winslow)?"
whispered the dying chief. "*Winsnow, matta
neen wonckanet namen* (Winslow, I shall never
see thee more)."

Winslow told Massasoit his friends in Plymouth were sorry to hear of his illness and that
the whole colony was praying for his recovery.

Massasoit shook his head slowly. He was
sure he could not get well. His mouth and throat
were so sore and swollen he could scarcely swal-

low. Even his eyes, his good keen eyes that could see a deer move before anyone else had seen it, now could not even see his friends.

Winslow opened his basket to take out the medicine and food that he had packed but, alas, found the precious bottles that he wanted most were broken. There was not a drop left in them! Only the jam jar had not spilled.

Winslow stuck his knife into the jam and laid a taste of it in Massasoit's mouth. "If you have someone who will go to Plymouth, I will write a note asking for medicine and for chickens to make broth," he offered. Messengers were quickly found who would start the long hike through the forests at once—even though it was two o'clock in the morning.

Winslow looked down at his friend and wished that he had something—anything—to feed him so as to bring back his strength. It would take much too long a time for the messengers to return.

There was no meat in the lodge, so he decided he would have to make Massasoit some soup with whatever was at hand. Looking around, he spied some corn in a large earthen bowl and asked one of the squaws to pound it into meal. When this was done he made a thin gruel. Outside the lodge he saw some young strawberry leaves, just poking their heads up through the straw. These and sassafras roots were all he could find to give flavor to the soup, which he had to strain through his handkerchief.

Massasoit drank this odd mixture eagerly, and asked for more. Maybe he was getting better! In a little while he began to recognize the friends who crowded about his couch. By the next day he was so much improved that he asked Winslow to shoot him a duck or a goose.

By the time the footsore messengers came back from Plymouth with the chickens and the medicine that the Pilgrims' doctor, Samuel Fuller, had prepared, Massasoit no longer needed medicine. And he would not let them kill the chickens. "I want to keep them so I can raise some more," he said.

Chickens seemed a priceless gift to the Indians

Chickens seemed a priceless gift to the Indians.

"Now I see the English are my friends and love me," Massasoit continued. "And as long as I live, I will never forget this kindness they have shown me."

And he never did. For as long as Massasoit lived, he and the Pilgrims were friends.

Chapter 7

MYLES STANDISH STRIKES

ABOUT THE TIME Edward Winslow and Hobomok returned from the visit to Massasoit, a con-
ference was being held in Plymouth. Bradford,
Brewster, Allerton, and Hopkins had gathered
in the Common House to discuss with Standish
what they should do about the rumor that the
Indians around Massachusetts Bay were planning to swoop down on Weston's colony at
Wessagusset and kill everybody.

Standish wanted to act fast. "If we don't
strike first, it may mean the end for all colonies."

Hopkins backed him up. "I think Standish is
right," he said.

Standish glanced around the group. He
knew that Allerton agreed with him, as well as

Hopkins. Brewster was shaking his head, dis-
agreeing. Governor Bradford was wavering,
chewing on his lip and gazing off into space. It
was hard for him to decide what was best.

"Once they have wiped out Wessagusset,
they will see how easy it is to get rid of any
settlement," Standish warned him. "If we allow
our neighbors at Wessagusset to be killed, even
though they are a disgrace to England, we will
be the next ones murdered. Indians everywhere
will see how easy it is to swoop down on a village and wipe it out."

The men finally decided that Standish and
eight armed men—all that Standish felt he dared
draw away from Plymouth at one time—should
set out at once for Wessagusset. When they
reached Weston's little settlement, they found
that the men there had sunk even lower than
they had feared. At first, the ruffians had abused
the Indians and stolen from them. Now, with all
food gone, they had become almost slaves to the
very Indians they had at first mistreated.

Standish pretended that he and his men were on a trading trip, but their secret was soon out.

Pecksuot, a tall and bold Indian, told the guides that the Indians were not fooled. "We know your little red captain is angry in his heart. He has come to kill us and not to trade with us as he pretends."

Then he strutted up to Standish himself and began to taunt him. "Though you are a great captain, you are but a small man. Even though I am no sachem, I am still a man of great strength and courage."

Later Pecksuot cornered Myles Standish a second time. He had Witawawmut with him, an Indian who had a burning hatred for all white men. Witawawmut, Pecksuot, and several of their friends squatted in a half circle before Standish. They pulled out their knives and began to stroke them lovingly.

"See what a fine knife this is," began Witawawmut. "See how sharp it is. But it is very thirsty . . ."

*The Indians stroked their knives lovingly as
Standish looked on*

Another picked up the story. "My knife, too, is sharp—and very, very thirsty. It wants to drink. And it likes to drink blood . . ."

Now it was Pecksuot's turn. "My knife has drunk both of English and French blood," he began, as he cuddled his weapon in his hand. "But today it is thirsty for English blood . . ."

Color rushed to Standish's face, but he held his temper for he knew this was no time to strike. He must wait until he could get Witawawmut, Pecksuot, and the others whose knives "wanted to drink deeply," alone in a hut.

Finally that moment arrived. With his own hands, Myles Standish stabbed Pecksuot to the heart. Witawawmut and two others were killed by some of Standish's men. It was a day of horror and one that the Pilgrims forever after wished that they could forget.

Several of the Wessagusset colonists decided to return with Standish to Plymouth. The rest gathered together their few possessions and sailed away north, toward the fishing grounds at Monhegan.

The story of the bloody slaughter at Wessagusset traveled from one tribe to another. If any
had been planning to join with the Massachusetts in an attack on the English, they at once
changed their minds.

Even the friendly Indians—those who had
been good neighbors—suddenly were filled with
dread. Many of them took to the swamps, hoping to hide where the little red captain, who
had such anger in his heart, could not find them.

Many Indians sickened and died from the
exposure. Among the dead were Aspinet and
laughing, kindly Iyanough, the Cape Cod sagamores who had rescued and cared for the
Billington boy who had been lost five days in
the woods during the first summer in America.

Wessagusset lay deserted. All that remained
to tell the story of Plymouth's first English
neighbor were a few half-finished shacks, some
logs, and the ashes of the campfires.

Chapter 8

HUNGRY DAYS

"VISITORS, VISITORS, and still more visitors—and not a one of them brings a bite to eat!" Worried Mother Brewster paused as she measured a tiny drop of corn mush into each wooden bowl. "No wonder we are almost down to our last bite."

"Mother, you know what would have happened if the colony had not shared, don't you? What else could we do?" Elder Brewster looked around at the hungry faces of his own family and of the children he and his wife had taken in as they were orphaned. "But if I'm not mistaken, there may be some changes around here in a few weeks. Will tells me that he has listened to just about all the grumbling he can take."

Governor Bradford knew that many of the grumblers were telling the truth. There were many people in the colony—even some of the original settlers who had come in the *Mayflower* —who were not doing their fair share of the work. And yet these people were the first to come running when the daily food was issued.

Just as he had done so many times before, when there were serious problems, Bradford called the leaders together. Old Elder Brewster, Isaac Allerton, Edward Winslow, Stephen Hopkins, Myles Standish, and a few more were the men with whom he felt he could talk freely and discuss what should be done.

"It is not right for our wives and children to have to work like slaves in the fields, as they have for the past two years, so that we can take care of all these extra mouths," said Hopkins.

"My wife says she is tired of washing clothes for this last batch of men, and cooking their meals," spoke up another. "I think it is about time we made some changes around here. If we don't, the women will mutiny."

All the men laughed, but became serious again very quickly.

"We must not forget that we are still in debt to the London merchants who advanced us money to get here," Bradford reminded them, as soon as the laughter died down. "It was a hard bargain they forced on us, but we agreed to keep our property in common for seven years and then to settle with our backers."

"Our mistake was in thinking that all men would do their fair share of work," said Brewster. "We have too many loafers in our midst who know that we will not let them starve."

"I think you are right," said Winslow. "Our trouble is in sharing alike. We made a bad mistake, I fear, when we agreed to pool everything that we have."

The men all nodded in agreement.

"Then, as I see it, there is but one answer to our problem." The governor was speaking again. "We must stop farming the land together. If each person is given his own small plot of land, perhaps everyone will be happier."

"At least the hard workers will be!" said Standish, laughing. "Those who have always worked will now feel that they are fairly treated. And the lazybones who are willing to live off other men's efforts will work or eat weeds!"

And so it was decided in the spring of 1623 that the governor should allot a strip of land to each family. Single men and boys were told they would have to join with some family and would be given as much land as they could till.

Working under the new scheme, the Pilgrims eagerly planted crops. More corn was set out than ever before. Women and children went willingly into the fields now that they knew they were working for themselves. Even the "lazybones" suddenly decided they would plant a garden. They still did not like to work—but they liked to eat.

Each day, until the new crops could be harvested, there would have to be smaller and smaller rations. By June, the food left from the year before was nearly gone. The men had become so weak that they staggered as they went to the fields. Their clothes hung on them like rags on a scarecrow.

The Pilgrims eagerly planted crops

Tired, hungry mothers wiped tears from their eyes when they thought no one was watching. They were worried most about their children whose little bodies had shrunk to skin and bones. Only their stomachs grew large, until it looked as if they would burst with the dreadful swelling that is a sign of starvation.

"If only we get a few good rains, we'll have nothing to worry about," the men who had once been Scrooby farmers told each other as they squinted up at the sky.

But the rains never came. Day after day the sun burned down from a cloudless sky, the leaves of the trees curled, and the grass turned brown. For six long weeks the parched earth felt scarcely a sprinkle.

The precious corn came up; then wilted. The stalks drooped and turned brown. Day after day the men scanned the horizon, praying for some sign of a storm. But no storm came.

A day of fasting and public prayer for rain was called for by the governor. That morning the sky was just as cloudless as it had been for many weeks.

Hobomok was surprised when he saw the Pilgrims setting out for their meeting house, for he knew it was not the Sabbath. He drew Myles Standish to one side. "Why is everyone going to the place where you talk with God?"

"To ask Him to give us rain," replied the captain.

Hobomok passed the word along that the Pilgrims were gathering to worship their Great Spirit and to ask Him to send rain.

The Indians watched and waited.

Hour after hour the Pilgrims prayed. Toward evening, clouds began to gather on all sides and the sky became overcast. By morning rain had come—soft, sweet, and gentle. For fourteen days and fourteen nights it rained, until the thirsty earth revived.

The Indians, watching the rain fall day after day, were sure, more than ever before, that the Pilgrims were under the special care of the Great Spirit who listened to their prayers.

Chapter 9

ARRIVAL OF THE "ANNE"
AND "LITTLE JAMES"

ABOUT THIS time a greedy sea captain put in to Plymouth in the *Plantation,* with several hogsheads of peas that he had brought to sell. When he saw how hungry the Pilgrims were, he asked a price for his peas that was many times their value.

The Pilgrims did not have the money to pay him, so he sailed on to Virginia with his cargo. But before he left, he mentioned to Governor Bradford that he had met a ship at sea that was on its way from England to Plymouth—the *Anne.* "Why, I even rowed over to her one day at sea to have a visit with her master, William Peirce. It seems strange that the *Anne* isn't here ahead of us," he said. "We got separated in a bad storm; I hope nothing has happened to her."

Two weeks slipped by, but still the *Anne* did not appear.

"What can have happened? Has she gone down with all on board during the storm in which she drifted far from the *Plantation?* Or has she been captured by pirates, a fate worse than drowning?" These were the questions on everyone's lips as anxious eyes scanned the horizon for a welcome sail.

People rushed to the beach to look for the ship

One morning a lookout gave a shout. People rushed to the beach, or to the highest points of land. Eyes strained to make out the ship. It was the *Anne*. She had not sunk, as many had begun to fear, but had simply drifted far off her course as she was buffeted about by a storm. Ten days after the *Anne* arrived, the *Little James* was sighted.

The *Anne* was a large ship, chartered for just one trip as the *Mayflower* and the *Fortune* had been. The *Little James* was a fishing vessel of only forty-four tons and had been built especially for the Pilgrims. Between them, the two ships brought nearly one hundred passengers, about sixty of whom had come to join the Pilgrims.

As the Pilgrims watched men, women, and children come ashore, disappointment showed on many faces. They knew so few of the new arrivals! John Robinson, the pastor from Leyden, was not among them. Many other loved faces did not appear. But at last the whole Brewster family was together again. Fear and

The Pilgrims and the newcomers were all disappointed

Patience, who had been left behind with friends in Leyden, had finally arrived.

The Pilgrims were not the only disappointed people. When the "Newcomers," as the people already there called them, stepped on land and saw the ragged men, women, and children who clustered round them, they could not believe their eyes. Surely these scarecrows could not be the same ones who had come over in the *Mayflower* and the *Fortune!* Why, these people were old, worn, gnarled; far worse than shabby. Some looked almost like Indians, standing half-naked in moccasins and tattered breeches. Clothing brought from England and Holland hung on gaunt frames in rags and patches.

One of the women began to cry. "I want to go home . . . I want to go back to England! They didn't tell me it would be like this," she sobbed as she turned to her husband's protecting arm.

Even the hardiest of the Newcomers had not expected to find the hardships the colonists faced. They could not believe that there had never been beef, or milk, or mutton on Plymouth tables. And now there was not even bread, and could be none until harvest.

The Newcomers had brought food with them. They were the first group to arrive, since those who came in the *Mayflower*, who had not had to beg food from the Pilgrims. Suddenly a terrible fear struck them. Maybe they would have to share the precious food they had brought from England with the Pilgrims. If they did not, the Pilgrims might starve.

The Old Settlers were just as worried. "These people have not learned to dole out their food to make it last," they thought. "They have plenty now, but they will gobble it down fast. Then next spring they'll come asking us to give them from our crop!" And so both groups agreed to eat what was theirs, and not to borrow or beg from the other.

If the people of Plymouth looked like scarecrows to the new arrivals, many of the Newcomers filled the Pilgrim leaders with equal dismay.

"We had a bad enough time with the Billingtons," Bradford confided later in the day to Standish, "but the Billingtons are nothing compared to some who arrived today! I'm afraid we are in for trouble."

"At least we can be thankful that about a third of them are our own families and friends," Elder Brewster reminded the two men.

But there were two Newcomers who Bradford and Standish were very glad had come. One was a girl named Barbara whom the fiery little captain married so quickly that nobody ever remembered her other name. The other was a young widow, Alice Southworth, who had left her two young boys with friends in Leyden. Soon she became Mrs. William Bradford.

Patience Brewster married Thomas Prence, the twenty-four-year-old carriage maker who had come in the *Fortune.* Her seventeen-year-old sister, Faith, married Isaac Allerton, a man nearly old enough to be her father, and became stepmother to Bartholomew, Remember, and Mary Allerton.

Chapter 10

WINSLOW WRITES A REPORT

FOR SIX WEEKS the Pilgrims cut lumber and loaded it, along with beaver skins, in the *Anne*. This cargo would help to pay off the colony's debts and to buy supplies that were always needed.

Edward Winslow was chosen to go to England with the shipment. Winslow spoke well, and the leaders felt that he would be the best one to report on the colony's progress to their creditors in England.

As Winslow embarked, he held under one arm a precious packet of papers. This was his report. He had tried several titles, scratching out first one, then another. Finally he had written in a clear, bold hand:

GOOD NEWES FROM NEW ENGLAND

*For six weeks the Pilgrims
cut lumber*

Winslow had worked many hours on his report before he embarked, writing it and then rewriting it. He had to be careful to tell the exact truth. Although life in the colony was hard and the Pilgrims were in great need, Winslow knew that he must write in such a way that men would still think Plymouth a good investment and be willing to lend them money. If they could get past the first few bad years, he felt sure they could stand on their own feet.

On calm days Winslow borrowed Captain Peirce's cabin and desk. Then his quill would scratch-scratch-scratch. Sometimes he wrote quickly; other times he would stop, wrinkle his brow, and blow on the feathers of his quill. This seemed to help him think, for in a minute or two he would cross out a word and begin to write once more.

The questions people will ask most will be about the Indians, he thought, remembering the false ideas the Pilgrims had of Indians before they had ever seen one. *I'm afraid the reports we sent back on the "Fortune" were not quite true, either. We had not been in Plymouth long enough, when we wrote them, to really know the Indians.*

He began to write:

A few things I think should be added which we have now observed about the Indians. Some of these things have to do with their religion and some with their customs.

At first we thought the Indians had no religion. We were mistaken as we know now that they do have a religion. They believe in many Divine Powers, the greatest of whom they call "Kiehtan."

In the beginning there were no kings, or Sachems, but only Kiehtan, the all-powerful spirit, who dwells above in the heavens where all good men go when they die. There, the Indians believe, they will see their friends and have their fill of all good things.

When the Indians want something badly, they gather and cry unto Kiehtan. And when they have received victory, or plenty—or whatever they have asked him for, they again meet and sing, dance, feast, and give thanks to Kiehtan.

Another Power the Indians worship, they call "Hobomok" or "Hobbamoqui." As far as we can make out, Hobomok could be called the Devil. They call upon him to cure their wounds and diseases. When the wounds or diseases are fatal, Hobomok tells the sufferers that Kiehtan is angry, so that none can cure.

This Hobomok appears in many forms to them. Sometimes he comes in the shape of a man, sometimes a deer, a fawn, an eagle, but most often . . . a snake.

The Devil does not make his appearances to everyone in the tribe, but just to the most important. One to whom he appears is a Powah, another is a Pinese. The main job of the Powah is calling upon the Devil and curing diseases and wounds. The Powah, when he calls to the Devil, looks fierce, makes many gestures, and talks wildly. If an Indian is wounded, the Powah will pretend that he is sucking the wound. Sometimes he says that an invisible eagle perched on his shoulder or a snake is doing the sucking.

The Indians use many sacrifices; and, in some cases, kill children. Not all Indians have the same customs. The Wampanoag Indians no longer worship Kiehtan as they once did, and say that they can remember the time when He was much more called upon.

The Narragansetts show much greater devotion, and have a great building into which only a few of their priests can go. To this house, at certain times, all the tribe go and offer almost all the riches they have to their gods: kettles, skins, hatchets, beds, knives. All these are cast by the priests into a great fire that they have made in the midst of the house, and are consumed to ashes. To this offering, every man bringeth freely and the more he is known to bring, the greater he is respected.

This custom is admired by other tribes who wish that their Sachems had them do the same. The plague has not touched the Narragansetts as it has the other tribes nearby and the Indians think that the Narragansetts have been spared because they sacrifice their possessions!

The Indians also believe that the Pineses of the tribe are in close contact with the Devil—Hobomok. Pineses are men of great courage and wisdom in the tribe who are highly thought of by all and are on the Sachem's Council. Without them, a Sachem will not go to war or undertake any weighty problem. They are commonly men of great height and strength, and will endure great hardship. They scorn theft, lying, and base dealings, and are as proud of having a good reputation as any of us.

It takes years of training to become a Pinese. The most promising boys are trained from childhood. They are made to go through many horrible and unpleasant tasks so that when they come of age, the Devil himself will appear to them.

All Indian Sachems cannot be called kings. Only a few of them are, to whom the rest turn for protection and pay homage. Massasoit, our friend, is one of these greater Sachems, or Sagamores. So is Canonicus, the Sachem of the Narragansetts whom we believe is our enemy.

Every Sachem takes care of the widows and the fatherless. He must also care for the old people and the injured and crippled if they have no friends or family to provide for them. A Sachem will not marry anyone who is not his equal in birth. They have many lesser wives but they are little more than servants and must take orders from the head wife. Indians, as a whole, observe this custom, not just the Sachems.

At this point, Winslow paused and read over

what he had written. *How much like our own customs are some of these customs of the Indian,* he thought. *Kings, princes, nobles . . .*

Once more he turned to his report:

Every Sachem knoweth how far the borders of his own country extend. Within his domain, he giveth any of his men who ask for land to plant in corn as much as they can use and sets boundaries on their plots. Whoever kills any venison within the land, must bring to the Sachem his "fee." This is the fore part of the deer if it was killed on land; but if it was killed in water, then the skin. . . .

All travelers or strangers, for the most part, lodge at the Sachem's . . .

Winslow shoved back his writing materials and gazed out at the sea. He was remembering his first visit to Massasoit. It was during the first summer at Plymouth and he, Stephen Hopkins, and Squanto had been sent by the Pilgrims to visit Massasoit at his headquarters in Sowams.

That was the time the Pilgrims sent him the copper chain, which he was to send with all his messengers, like a secret password, in order that the people in Plymouth would know the messenger really did come from Massasoit. It was the only way they could think of to cut down on the number of Indian visitors they were having. *If I hadn't thought of that chain, we would probably have had every Wampanoag in the land "drop in" for a meal and a visit!*

Now Winslow could smile as he remembered that trip to Sowams. They had lodged at the sachem's just as he had written in his report. *But how different this will sound when read in England,* he said to himself, chuckling. *I don't dare write that visiting the sachem means sleeping six to a bed—not counting the lice, fleas, and mosquitoes that are always uninvited guests!*

Winslow picked up his quill and began to write once more:

Once a year the Pineses carry on a drive to get the people to give corn to the Sachem. They set a certain time and place. The place is always near the Sachem's dwelling where the people can make a great stack of corn. The Pineses stand at the place where the corn is to be placed, prepared to thank each person who gives of his crop on the Sachem's behalf.

When Indians are sick, their friends come to cheer them, and stay with them until they die or recover. If they die, the friends stay awhile to mourn for them. Night and morning, they perform this duty in a most doleful manner which makes them cry—and almost brings tears to our eyes, too. But if they get well, they receive gifts and the Indians hold a feast and dance, which they call Commoco.

When Indians bury their dead, they sew up the corpse in a mat, and put it in the earth. If the dead person is a Sachem, they cover him with many unusual mats, and bury all his riches with him and put a fence around the grave.

If it be a child, the father will also put his own best ornaments in the earth with it. The father will also cut his hair and disfigure himself very much as a token of his sorrow. If it be the man or woman of the house, the rest of the family will pull down the mats which form the walls of the house, leaving only the frame standing and bury them in or near the frame.

The Indians we have met employ themselves wholly in hunting and other exercises of the bow; except sometimes they take some pains in fishing. The women live a most slavish life. They carry all the men's burdens, set and hoe their corn, gather it in, hunt for much of the food, make ready the corn to eat, and have all household cares.

Indian young people revere the elder and do all the unpleasant tasks when they are together, even though they be strangers. Boys and girls may not wear their hair like men and women.

A man is not accounted a man until he does some notable act, or shows great courage. Men take much tobacco; but for boys to do so, they do not approve. All their names have meaning and may be changed. When they become men and women, they alter them, according to their deeds and their dispositions!

Thinking back to the time when Massasoit had sent Governor Bradford his own knife to cut off Squanto's head and hands when Squanto had offended him, Winslow wrote:

In matters of unjust and dishonest dealings, the Sachem investigates and punishes the guilty. In cases of theft, an Indian is scolded for the first offense, beaten on the back with a cudgel for the second, and has his nose slit for the third. If any Indian kill another, he must likewise be killed.

The Sachem not only passes the sentence, but performs the executions with his own hands. If the person to be executed is not present, the Sachem will send his own knife, so that another can perform the execution.

With the exception of execution, all punishments are given out by the Sachem himself. An Indian never tries to run away from punishment, and it is considered a worse disgrace to cry out with pain when being punished than it was to do whatever he had done which brought on the punishment.

Indians are clever and observant. They keep account of time by the moon and by the seasons. They know a number of the stars by name. They call the North Star "Maske," which means "The Bear" and they have many names for the winds. They are able to guess very well at wind and weather beforehand.

They have a difficult language with many words. And even now, after three years, we cannot understand or speak it very well. But Indians of different tribes—even ones 100 miles apart—seem able to understand each other.

Hour after hour, day after day, Edward Winslow toiled on. Sometimes he found it too rough and stormy to work on his reports. Then he would hunch down in his cloak to keep warm, and think of the little colony at Plymouth whose future depended upon him.

Chapter 11

SECRET LETTERS

ONE YEAR, two years, three years slipped by, and still Plymouth had no minister. Each ship that arrived brought fresh disappointment to the colony when they found the beloved pastor, John Robinson, and his family were not on board.

The Pilgrims who had not come from Leyden or Scrooby felt by this time that they knew John Robinson almost as well as did his own congregation. They had listened many times to the story of the secret church services in Scrooby Manor, Elder Brewster's old home in England. They had heard how the people of Scrooby for years had dodged the King's officers, moving their secret church services from manor house to barns and lofts. They could see, almost as if they had been there, John Robinson reading the Bible by moonlight at these services, when it seemed too dangerous even to light a candle.

Many times, too, they had heard the Scrooby Pilgrims tell of the flight from England and how the helpless boat, with seasick women and children, became stuck fast in the mud. They knew how the Scrooby people managed to reach Amsterdam and how they moved from there to Leyden a year later, where the big old house, known as the "Green Gate," became their headquarters.

John Robinson and his wife and children lived in the upper part of this house; church services had been held in the lower rooms. They had planned, step by step, the journey to America. Then, when John Robinson discovered how few families in his congregation were willing to accept the harsh terms of their London backer, Thomas Weston, the Green Gate pastor decided to remain for the time being with the greater number of his "flock" in Leyden. He would come over later. This he promised.

But he never came.

"What has happened?" anxious Pilgrims would ask each other as each ship arrived without Robinson.

"Can he have changed his mind? He promised us . . ." people would say to each other after every ship arrived.

"If only he would come now when we need him so much."

It was all right for Elder Brewster to lead services until John Robinson could get to Plymouth, but Brewster could not go on taking their beloved pastor's place forever. Still Robinson did not come, and no one was ever quite sure of the reason why.

Then one day in March, 1624, a mysterious stranger arrived who claimed to be a minister. His name was John Lyford, but nobody in the colony knew anything about him—not even Edward Winslow who returned from a trip to England in the same ship in which Lyford arrived.

Another mysterious person who had come into the colony a little earlier was John Oldham, or "Mad Jack" Oldham, as he was later known. He was a mean, blustering brute of a man who went into screaming rages.

The Pilgrims, when they welcomed Lyford and Oldham, did not know that they were welcoming spies who wanted to wreck the colony.

The two men at once began to make trouble, holding secret meetings with men like John Billington. At the same time, they pretended to be loyal, true friends of the Pilgrims. They lived in their homes and ate their food. But as soon as they had finished eating a Pilgrim meal, they would sneak away to work on secret "reports," to be sent to the men in England who had backed the little colony.

Lyford seemed to be everywhere. One minute he was poking about in the weeds or peering into windows, the next sneaking up behind people to listen to private conversations.

"There is something rotten going on around here," Bradford whispered to Edward Winslow one day when they were too far away for even a spy to read their lips.

Lyford peered into windows

"I have had the same feeling for some time," confessed Winslow, "but what can we do? I am beginning to think there are at least two people in Plymouth who are not what they pretend to be . . ."

"Wait. If you mean what I think you mean, we had better keep a sharp eye on both Oldham and Lyford! If we are clever, perhaps we can catch them red-handed."

Days and weeks went by. The two spies did not know it, but they were being watched every moment. Slowly, carefully, Bradford and Winslow were building up their evidence, for they had to be sure of the men's guilt. Day after day Lyford handed a thick letter to the ship's captain to be taken back to England when he sailed.

"Something tells me those are not really letters, but are secret reports," Bradford said to Winslow on the day the *Charity* was planning to leave. "If they are reports, I am going to get them."

Toward dusk, when the *Charity* started her long voyage, Governor Bradford and a small party put out in the shallop to accompany the ship to sea. This was a common way of saying farewell, so nobody thought anything of it.

But when it grew dark, and the shallop had not come back, some of the Pilgrims began to worry, looking out over the dark sea for some sign of their friends. Oldham and Lyford, whose guilty consciences were bothering them, began to quake in their boots. Finally, late at night, the shallop returned. Bradford, and those who had gone with him, made no explanation.

Lyford and Oldham would have quaked even more, had they known what had been going on during the hours the shallop was at sea. The captain of the *Charity*, who was a friend of the Pilgrims, had turned over to Bradford all the letters written by the two men. Oldham, who could scarcely sign his name, had sent only a few miserable scrawls, but there were more than twenty great thick letters, in John Lyford's handwriting, to be inspected.

Bradford and his helpers read every letter. The governor did not like to read other men's letters. But it was a job that had to be done for the safety of the colony. Most of the letters they simply copied so that the colony would have a record of them. A few of the worst ones—so bad that Bradford felt Lyford would deny ever having written them—were kept, and careful copies were made to send to England.

"I'm better with a gun than a pen," growled Myles Standish, as he tried to help Bradford with the copying.

The day after the shallop's return nothing happened. Nothing happened the next day, or the day following. Slowly Lyford and Oldham began to relax. They did not know that Bradford was waiting, biding his time.

Finally the right moment came for exposing the two traitors, and Governor Bradford called a general meeting of the colonists. Everyone wondered what the meeting was for; nobody seemed to know. Oldham and Lyford both appeared and boldly sat in the front row, ready to make trouble if they saw a chance.

Every face turned toward Bradford.

"I think it only fair to tell you something that several of us have known for some time," he began. "We have spies and traitors in Plymouth. They pretend to be our friends, they eat our bread, they live in our homes, and yet every minute of the day they are plotting against us. Their names"—here Bradford paused—"their names are Lyford and Oldham!"

"You dirty liar!" shouted Oldham and began to curse Bradford with oaths so vile that even Myles Standish gasped.

"What you say is not true," snapped Lyford, who had better manners than his companion. "You are the ones who are traitors."

"Let the people decide," Bradford stated in a quiet voice. "Maybe they can decide better if they hear your letters," he said, holding up a packet for all to see. Then, one by one, Bradford read the letters of the two traitors aloud, letters so packed with lies about the colony and its leaders that the people were stunned. When he had finished the last letter, there was complete silence.

Lyford hung his head in shame, but Oldham lashed back at Bradford. He leaped to his feet and called on everyone in the colony who did not like the way things were run to come to his aid.

Not a man, woman, or child spoke up.

Then Bradford reminded them that no one was a slave in Plymouth. "Speak up if you have any complaints," he said. Then, turning to one of the worst troublemakers in the colony, Bradford continued, "All right, Billington, I know you are in on this. Suppose we hear from you first."

All eyes shifted to John Billington, who squirmed and shuffled to his feet. Pointing toward Lyford he whined, "That one there fed me a pack of lies. I am going to stick."

"How about you?" asked Bradford, turning to the man next to Billington.

"Me too," promised another of Lyford and Oldham's friends.

This was more than John Oldham could stand. He lunged at the man. "Say what you

John Oldham lunged at the man

really think!" he roared. "You weren't so chicken-livered an hour ago!"

Nearly everyone of Lyford and Oldham's followers deserted them when given a chance to speak out. Lyford, who was cleverer than Oldham, kept his head down. But Oldham roared like a madman and had to be held under guard until he could be expelled from the colony.

By keeping his mouth shut, Lyford got a second chance. But in a short time, he was asked to leave Plymouth. He went north about thirty miles to Nantasket—the new settlement Oldham had started. Today it is called Hull.

Chapter 12

FATE OF THE "LITTLE JAMES"

THE SUMMER of 1625 was nearly over. Soft breezes rustled through the corn, and bees buzzed happily as they worked, storing up honey for the long winter to come. Little Peregrine White, the *Mayflower* baby who survived, watched the bees at their work. He would soon be five years old. Young as he was, he could sense that something was wrong. He had seen his stepfather, Edward Winslow, talking in worried tones to his mother many times that summer.

No wonder Edward Winslow was worried. The colony was in great trouble. By 1625 nobody was starving; this time the problem was money. It seemed that anything the Pilgrims tried to do to earn a living sooner or later failed.

The December before, when their salt-works burned, the colony's London backers had thrown up their hands in disgust and said they were through—absolutely, completely through! "Better to lose what we have already sunk in Plymouth, than to go on pouring good money into something we know is doomed."

Governor Bradford tried not to let the people see how desperate he felt. "We have to raise money somewhere, have to get more supplies. But where can we turn?" he asked Winslow.

"Men everywhere respect Standish; perhaps he is the one to send to England this time," Winslow suggested. "If anyone in the colony can get a loan, he can."

Myles Standish hated the thought of making the trip to England. Only six years before, the New World had seemed a far-off wilderness. Now it was home, and England seemed the faraway, distant place.

In a few weeks, two ships were being made ready to sail. One was the large and fast *Jacob;* the other was the colony's little pinnace, the

James, which seemed to carry its own bad luck wherever it went. Loading grew louder and noisier as the two ships' captains fought over the cargo of fish and furs.

"These skins are worth a fortune!" bellowed the captain of the *Jacob.* "Anybody in his right mind knows they should go in a ship and not in a miserable little tub. Why, you've already gone to the bottom once!"

The red-faced, angry captain of the pinnace fought back. "This cargo has been promised me. It is mine by rights," he insisted.

Standish, and most of the Pilgrims watching the fight, secretly agreed with the captain of the *Jacob,* but there was nothing they could do. Edward Winslow had said that the furs must go in the *James,* for the agreement he had made in England required it.

The quarrel continued until Governor Bradford was called upon to decide. He could say only that Winslow's agreement had to be carried out, for their honor was at stake.

Even though the Pilgrim furs went in the

pinnace, Standish chose to cross the Atlantic in the larger, safer, more comfortable ship whose captain consented to tow the little *James* because of its valuable cargo.

All went well as they crossed the Atlantic and entered the English Channel. Then the towline was cut and the *James* was allowed to drop behind, for the ships were going into different ports. It did not look as if any harm could come to the little pinnace and her cargo during the last few miles. Then, to everyone's horror, a pirate sail suddenly appeared in the distance. Larger and larger grew the pirate ship as it gained on them.

Standish wanted to turn back to help the tiny *James*.

"I cannot," said his ship's captain. "Do you want to be captured, too? I am not strong enough to do battle, so if I turn back, we would both be lost." The *Jacob* bounded ahead and left the little *James* to her dreadful fate.

When the *Jacob* reached Portsmouth, a city on the south coast of England, Standish heard six months' news. He was told that King James I, the king who had tried to stop Scrooby farmers from going to Holland nearly twenty years before, had died in March. His son Charles I was on the throne. "King Charles is making England an even unhappier place than it was under his father," Puritan friends warned Standish.

He learned, too, that John Robinson was dead. Standish knew what heartbreaking news this would be for the Pilgrims from Leyden.

As he headed for London, he gazed in amazement at the villages. *How neat and tiny all of England looks! I had almost forgotten how pretty little gardens are after our wild New England fields.*

Near the city, he met many people fleeing with all their possessions, for London was in the clutches of the great plague of 1625. Ceaselessly, carts rolled past him, piled high with pots, pans, bedding, and babies. Some of the people who were escaping from the city did not know they were carrying the dread disease with them. Soon they would die in the villages where they stopped. In London, Standish saw many empty houses—gaunt and forlorn. Some of them were houses of death, marked with the sign of the plague.

In spite of the danger, Standish did his best to find James Sherley, one of the colony's few backers who had seemed friendly. Sherley was not at his home near London and the neighbors

No one guessed that the thousands of rats were carrying the disease

said that he had not been seen for some time. Nobody knew where he had gone.

Meanwhile, Standish was finding it harder and harder to get food or a place to sleep. He found it nearly as hard to borrow money, even with interest of fifty percent.

All London lived in terror that winter, for people did not know what caused the plague. They did not know whether they should hold something over their faces to keep out the deadly disease or if it was safe to breathe the city air. They did not even know whether it was safe to touch anything that others had touched or to eat food they had handled.

Some people were sure the plague lay hidden in the ground, just as Squanto had told the Indians it did at Plymouth when he wanted to frighten them. Others said it must be in the water, or the air, or the food they ate. In all of London, there was not one person who guessed that the thousands of rats, scurrying in and out of houses, barns, and drains, were carrying the dread disease wherever they went.

Chapter 13

SOME GOOD AND NOT-SO-GOOD NEIGHBORS

NOT MANY months after the men of Weston's colony sailed away, a group, led by Robert Gorges, arrived from England and set up a trading post near the ruins of Wessagusset. The Gorges colony was small, but the men had brought good equipment, servants, and laborers. When this colony failed, the men spread out, setting up little trading huts here and there along the coast. Thomas Walford chose a spot on Massachusetts Bay that later became Charlestown. William Blackstone settled in what is now the heart of Boston. Samuel Maverick made his base on the north side of the Mystic River in Chelsea. Still another decided he liked Maine better than Massachusetts and headed north.

David Thompson, who was a friend of the

Gorges family, received a grant of "six thousand acres and an island." Thompson chose land in New Hampshire for his "six thousand acres" and, for his island, picked the one the Pilgrims had earlier named "Trevore."

Trading posts now were springing up thick and fast.

One group planned a base where fishermen could winter in safety, and began to build huts on Cape Ann. Three of the men who joined the Cape Ann settlement were well known to the Pilgrims. They were John Oldham and John Lyford, who had been expelled from Plymouth, and Roger Conant, who had left the colony at the time of their trouble. The Pilgrims had no reason to think better of them than they had before, for the men at Cape Ann seized a fishing pier at Gloucester that the Pilgrims had worked hard to build.

The Cape Ann colony failed, and Lyford took many of the settlers with him to Virginia. Others, discouraged by the hardships in the New World, went back to England. But Roger

Conant, who had become governor of the Cape Ann colony, was made of sterner stuff. He hated to see the little colony disappear, so he gathered a few of the strongest and best men and their families and moved them, in 1626, to a new base a few miles away on Massachusetts Bay. This new settlement they named Naumkeag. Today it is called Salem.

While the Cape Ann settlement was having its troubles, new neighbors arrived. They came with a Captain Wollaston in 1625 and set up a trading post not far from where Weston's and Robert Gorges' small settlements lay in ruins. The men who had come with Wollaston were wealthy and influential and had plenty of money and supplies and many indentured servants— men who had agreed to labor a certain number of years to pay for their passage.

After one unhappy year in Massachusetts, Captain Wollaston became so discouraged that he took most of his men to Virginia. Only about ten were left at Mt. Wollaston in charge of a Lieutenant Fitcher and Thomas Morton.

In no time at all, Morton had ousted Fitcher from the colony and was in command. Then, when Wollaston sent word for the rest of his men to join him in Virginia, Morton saw an easy way to trick Wollaston out of his laborers and get a colony of his own started without any cost.

"You are fools if you go to Virginia," he told Wollaston's indentured workers. "You still have many years to work for Wollaston. If you go to Virginia, you will be no better off than slaves."

When he saw the men were beginning to weaken, he put more bait in his trap. "Forget about Wollaston. Stay here with me and we can have our own colony, Mare Mount. We shall all be partners!"

The men stayed.

Morton loved gayety — singing, dancing, drinking, and carnivals. He looked down his nose at the sober, hard-working Pilgrims and made fun of them. On May Day he built a Maypole eighty feet high and topped it with a buck's horns. When he got the pole decked with flowers, he said it was silly for a group of men to dance

around a Maypole alone. "Come dance with us,"
he coaxed the Indians, and offered them strong
drink.

"Come dance with us," he coaxed the Indians

The Pilgrims were shocked by what was going on at "Merry" Mount, as they now began to call Morton's colony. Worst of all, Morton was paying the Indians for their furs with guns and powder. This could mean death for all the colonists of New England. In many ways, little settlements here and there along the coast of Massachusetts, New Hampshire, and Maine were rivals. But on one question they all agreed: there must be no selling of guns and powder to Indians.

"If we band together and share the cost, we can get rid of this 'Merry' nuisance," the Pilgrims suggested.

Almost every settlement sent money to Governor Bradford, who carefully wrote down the amount in his letter-book.

Myles Standish then marched with a few men to "Merry" Mount and seized the drunken Morton and his revelers. Morton was put on a boat and sent to England. All that was left of "Merry" Mount was a Maypole with a few tattered streamers still dangling from it.

Chapter 14

DUTCH NEIGHBORS COME TO CALL

GOVERNOR BRADFORD had called a meeting of his council. They had money problems to discuss. No matter how hard the Pilgrims worked, they never seemed able to get out of debt. Each year the sum owed grew larger and larger.

Several years before, Weston had sold his interest in the colony to some of the other backers in London, so the colonists no longer had him to worry about. But some of the other creditors were asking fifty percent interest and the leaders knew that things could not go on this way forever.

After many hours' discussion they agreed to send Isaac Allerton to England to arrange a final settlement with all their creditors.

Allerton's mission was successful and, on

October 26, 1626, the men in London made over to the Pilgrims all their shares, lands, personal possessions, and merchandise. Everything the Pilgrims had managed to obtain in six years of hard work in the New World was to be theirs.

In return the colony had to pay 1,800 pounds sterling, at the rate of 200 pounds a year, starting in 1628. Bradford, Brewster, Standish, Winslow, and Allerton of the older Pilgrims, and Alden, Howland, and Prence, who were still in their twenties, signed an agreement stating that they would be personally responsible for the debt. From that day on, the colony was on its own.

One of the first things the leaders did, after signing the new agreement, was to build a pinnace on Buzzard's Bay. They had found the long trip around Cape Cod dangerous in a small boat and had seen how easy it would be to portage their wares the few miles between Plymouth and Buzzard's Bay. They built a trading post at Aptucxet.

The Dutch, who had been settling along the Hudson River since 1626, sent friendly letters of greeting to the Pilgrims. Their governor, Peter Minuit, wanted to trade with them. In September, 1627, Governor Bradford received a message from the secretary of the Dutch colony, Isaack DeRasieres, saying that he was at Buzzard's Bay and would like to visit Plymouth.

What hustling and bustling went on in some of the homes in Plymouth that day! It had been seven long years since the Leyden Pilgrims had had a chance to use the Dutch language. "Do you suppose we can remember the words?" they anxiously asked each other as they tried to talk Dutch again.

The guests from Fort Amsterdam stayed with the Pilgrims several days. When finally it came time for them to leave, some of the Pilgrims went back with them to their pinnace and bought the sugar, linen, and other articles that the Dutch had brought for trading.

One of the articles DeRasieres had brought was Wampumpeag, a strange kind of Indian money that he said the tribes on Long Island Sound and to the north of his trading post were using. It was made from small pieces of white and purple shell that had been carefully ground and polished.

DeRasieres told the puzzled Pilgrims, when they examined it, that the Indians strung wampum like beads and wore it when not using it for trade. The Pilgrims bought some of this strange shell money from him, and then, for a long time, could not get rid of it.

Massasoit and some of his people had seen Wampumpeag, but they had never used it. Many Indians felt of it, but it was two years before the Pilgrims could find anyone willing to trade for it.

As time went on, both Indians and colonists came to use it as money for small purchases in Plymouth, and the Pilgrims wondered how they had ever managed before DeRasieres had shown them these strange Indian "coins."

Sometime later, DeRasieres wrote a letter to his employers in Holland, for he knew they would be anxious to know what life was like in Plymouth.

. . . New Plymouth lies on the slope of a hill stretching east towards the seacoast, with a broad street about a cannon shot of 800 yards long, leading down the hill; with a crossing in the middle, northwards to the rivelet, and southwards to the land. The houses are constructed of hewn planks, with gardens also inclosed behind and at the sides with hewn planks, so that their houses and courtyards are arranged in very good order, with a stockade, against a sudden attack; and at the ends of the streets there are three wooden gates.

In the centre, on the cross street, stands the Governor's house, before which is a square inclosure upon which four patereros [called "murderers" by the English because, instead of a single ball, they were loaded with broken pieces of iron and stone that spread as the guns were shot] are mounted, so as to flank along the streets. Upon the hill, they have a large square house, with a flat roof, made of thick sawn planks, stayed with oak beams, upon the top of which they have six cannons, which shoot iron balls of four and five pounds, and command the surrounding country. The lower part they use for their church, where they preach on Sundays and the usual holidays.

They assemble by beat of drum, each with his musket or firelock, in front of the captain's door; they have their cloaks on and place themselves in order, three abreast, and are led by a sergeant without beat of drum. Behind comes the Governor, in a long robe;

*The Governor, the Preacher, and the Captain are
led by a sergeant, without beat of drum*

beside him, on the right hand, comes the Preacher with his cloak on, and on the left hand the Captain with his side arms and cloak on, and with a small cane in his hand—and so they march in good order, and each sets his arms down near him. Thus they are constantly on their guard night and day.

Their farms are not so good as ours [at New Amsterdam], because they are more stony . . . The maize seed which they do not require for their own use is delivered over to the Governor, at three guilders the bushel, who in his turn sends it in sloops to the north for the trade in skins among the savages. They reckon one bushel of maize against one pound of beaver's skin . . .

They have better means of living than we do, because they have fish so abundant before their doors. There are also many birds, such as geese, herons, and cranes, and other small-legged birds, which are in great abundance there in the winter. The tribes in their neighborhood have the same customs as I have already described, only they are better behaved than ours because the English give them the example of better laws and a better life . . .

Chapter 15

THE GREAT MIGRATION

Six months after Isaack DeRasieres' visit to the Pilgrims, the Massachusetts Bay Company, in England, received from the Council for New England, a patent to set up a colony.

Many wealthy and influential English families had become "Puritans," as the people were called who wanted to reform the Church of England and make its laws more strict. Because of this, the government was making life increasingly hard for Puritans in England, and many of them had decided to take their servants and families to America. Since so many wanted to leave, the Massachusetts Bay Company planned to send many groups in many ships. They dreamed of a great Puritan colony in the New World.

John Endicott was appointed leader of the first group. With some Puritan colonists and some of the servants of those who planned to come later, he sailed in the *Abigail* from Weymouth, England, in the summer of 1628. In the early fall they reached Naumkeag, Roger Conant's two-year-old settlement on Massachusetts Bay. They found Conant and his "Old Planters" camped out in a few wattle huts that had dirt floors and thatched roofs.

"Any luck?" Conant whispered anxiously to one of the passengers from the *Abigail* as soon as he could draw him to one side. The man was John Woodbury, one of Conant's own "planters," who had gone to England to beg aid for Conant's tiny colony and had been fortunate enough to get passage back in the *Abigail* for himself and his son.

The man shook his head and Conant listened with dismay to his story. "There will be no more help. Our backers have deserted us and turned over any interest they have in us to the Massachusetts Bay Company."

As far as John Endicott was concerned, Conant and the thirty-five people living around him were "squatters"—people who had no right to be where he intended to settle.

Like the Pilgrims at Plymouth ten years before, the Endicott party arrived as winter was setting in, and had to work fast to get shelters built at Naumkeag. Many of them were already suffering from scurvy and fever. Endicott appealed to Plymouth for help. The Pilgrims proved themselves good neighbors; they sent their own doctor, Samuel Fuller, to Naumkeag to help care for the sick and dying. He stayed with them several months.

Endicott did the best he could, but the Massachusetts Bay Company had asked too much of his little colony in expecting it to have a thriving village established by the time the next party arrived.

The Massachusetts Bay Company's second group was sent out in the spring of 1629 in the *Talbot, George, Lion's Whelp, Four Sisters,* and a fifth ship bearing the same name as the Pilgrims' ship, the *Mayflower*.

In the ten years since the Pilgrims' arrival at Cape Cod, people had learned more about the things they should take with them on a sea journey and what route to follow. However, men still had to face dangers in crossing the ocean that they could not prepare for in advance.

Soon after sailing, the *Talbot* sighted a man-of-war. As those on board waited for the dreadful moment when it would turn and give chase, they longed to be back home in England. The captain of the pirate ship decided not to risk an attack, for he saw the *Lion's Whelp* close by.

Before the passengers had time to recover from this scare, a terrible storm arose. When mountainous waves broke over the decks, even the sailors were afraid. Trembling passengers, huddled below, could hear the hoarse voices of the crew as they shouted to each other to make fast the long boat and batten down the hatches.

Having come safely out of the storm, off

Newfoundland the *Talbot* and *Lion's Whelp* ran into fog so thick it settled down on them like a fluffy, white blanket. Fog was everywhere! The two ships began to drift apart, and anxious men tried shooting off guns in a desperate effort to keep in touch. It was too late—already the ships

A terrible storm arose

were too far apart for sound to carry from one to the other. Each one was now on its own. To add to the troubles, smallpox broke out on the *Talbot*. One member of the crew and one of the children died.

When the *Talbot* finally worked its way out of the Newfoundland fog banks, the skies began to clear and it was possible to pick up the *Lion's Whelp* once more.

By the time the two ships reached Cape Ann, it was the middle of summer. Francis Higginson, a minister on board the *Talbot*, was amazed by the beauty of Massachusetts.

"As we sailed along the coasts," he wrote, "we saw every hill and dale and every island full of gay woods and high trees. The nearer we came to the shore, the more flowers there were in abundance, sometimes scattered abroad, sometimes jointed in sheets nine or ten yards long, which we suppose were brought from the low meadows by the tide."

The fog dropped again, but the next morning it "burned off" and by late afternoon the *Tal-*

bot and *Lion's Whelp* saw a fine harbor seven miles from the tip of Cape Ann. Four men went ashore in a small boat and brought back strawberries, gooseberries, and roses.

As the ships approached Naumkeag, John Endicott anxiously tried to identify them; there was always the possibility that they might belong to some unfriendly nation. As soon as he could make out their English colors, he sent two men out in his shallop to lead them through the winding and twisting passage into Naumkeag.

As soon as the *Talbot* and *Lion's Whelp* were in the harbor, those on board saw a sight that made them cheer. The *George,* which had left England a week before they had, and which carried most of their cattle, horses, and goats, already lay at anchor. Within a few weeks, the *Four Sisters* and the *Mayflower* also appeared.

The ships were loaded with arms, tools, and equipment. Among those who arrived in the summer of 1629 were many laborers and artisans —coopers, shoemakers, boat builders, and carpenters—who were expected to get industries started before the main group of colonists came the next year.

While the first and second groups were busily at work in the New World, the Massachusetts Bay Company was busy in England preparing the *Arbella, Talbot, Ambrose,* and *Jewell* for the third and still larger expedition the next year. John Winthrop, who had been chosen governor of the colony while still in England, was to take charge of the third group. He planned to sail in the largest and most important ship of the convoy, the *Arbella*. This ship had been called the *Eagle,* but was renamed to honor the daughter of the Earl of Lincoln. Lady Arbella was going as a colonist with her husband, Isaac Johnson.

Many well-to-do Puritan families planned to sail with Governor Winthrop and they were busy getting together the best food and supplies that money could buy.

Although the Winthrop convoy left England in the spring, it ran into storm after storm. When people were seasick, the leaders used a strange remedy to make them well. They forced all who were stretched out moaning in their bunks to get up and go on deck. Those who were too weak to crawl up the ladders on their own were dragged and pushed.

"Hang to the rope!" came the command as soon as each one staggered into the open.

As soon as he had clutched the rope that was strung the length of the deck, a second order came. "Now jump up and down until you feel warm and happy!"

The colonists had not only the dangers of the ocean crossing to face, but also the hardships of beginning a new life in America. When Winthrop's convoy reached Naumkeag, the governor learned that about eighty people had died the winter before and many who survived were still sick and weak. In spite of the generous supplies the first two groups had carried, there was scarcely enough food left in Naumkeag to last two weeks. Taking this as a warning that his group, too, might run short before their first harvest, Winthrop sent a ship back to England as fast as it could go to bring more provisions.

"Hang on to the rope," came the command

Winthrop did not like Naumkeag, and began almost at once to look around for a better place to settle. He took a few friends and hiked south along the shores of Massachusetts Bay, carefully considering some of the same meadows and riverbanks that the Pilgrims had explored and thought beautiful in 1621.

Winthrop decided on Charlestown. Sir Richard Saltonstall and George Phillips explored the shallow Charles River and decided to move inland a few miles. They named their settlement Watertown.

Still another group of Puritans—who had arrived several weeks ahead of Winthrop's fleet—had already started a village near the mouth of the Neponset River, called Dorchester.

Winthrop's settlers had not been long at Charlestown when they realized that they had made a bad mistake. Charlestown was not a good place for a village, after all. It had only one spring and that spring could not be used at high tide. Many people were ill; Lady Arbella had already died.

A short distance across the mouth of the Charles River, the strange, hermit-like William Blackstone lived all by himself in a shack on the wooded peninsula that he called Trimountaine and the Indians called Shawmut. Blackstone rowed over to see the newcomers. He bragged about Trimountaine because it had three hills that looked like small, pointed mountains, and said it was much better than Charlestown.

"I never run short of water," he told Winthrop. "Why, it bubbles out of the ground all the time! There are many springs where I live. Come over; there is room enough for all of us."

When Winthrop visited Trimountaine, he agreed with Blackstone that it was the finest location on Massachusetts Bay. Again he moved his colony; this time from Charlestown to a spot not far from Blackstone's home.

On the seventeenth of September, 1630, the name Trimountaine was changed to Boston.

Chapter 16

TROUBLE WITH THE INDIANS

As THE YEARS passed and English settlements grew, the colonists needed more and more land. They bought it from the Indians, but, to the Indians, "selling" meant only sharing. When the Wampanoags saw their hunting grounds fenced in as farms, they wanted them back. "The English have cut down our forests so the deer no longer come," they complained.

"They are not your forests and fields any longer," Massasoit reminded his people. "Remember, you *sold* your lands to the Englishmen."

But the Indians did not want to remember. The beads and the blankets, the knives and trinkets were all broken or worn out, and the money given them was spent, but the land was still there, looking more beautiful than it had ever looked before.

"The English have cheated us," angry Indians cried over and over to Massasoit. "Let us drive them out of the land of Pokanoket forever!"

But Massasoit never forgot the treaty he had "talked out" with the Pilgrims the first time he met them. "They are our friends," he reminded his tribes. "They have paid us for our lands. They have kept their promises to us and we must keep our promises to them."

As long as Massasoit was alive, the Wampanoag Indians and the people of Plymouth Colony did remain friends.

As the years passed, new faces appeared among the leaders of the colony, for those who had come in the *Mayflower* grew old and died. By 1657, Elder Brewster, Edward Winslow, Myles Standish, and Governor Bradford were dead. Thomas Prence succeeded Bradford as governor of Plymouth, and Edward Winslow's son Josiah became military leader. Finally a day came in 1661 when Massasoit himself lay still in death. His son Wamsutta, whose name in the Indian language means "a warm and loving heart," became Sachem.

Wamsutta went to Plymouth with his younger brother Pometacom, to renew agreements with the colony. The two men at that time asked the Pilgrims for English names; Wamsutta became "Alexander" and Pometacom became "Philip."

Not long afterward a rumor was started that Alexander was plotting against Apaum, the Indian name for Plymouth. Harsh Governor Prence, who was not as tactful as Governor Bradford had been, sent word to Alexander to come at once to Plymouth.

When Alexander, the ruler of the Wampanoags, failed to appear, Governor Prence ordered Major Josiah Winslow to go after him. "Take an armed force, if need be, and get him; I want to question him."

Alexander became very ill while with the Pilgrims and died as he was being carried home. Indians soon after began to say that he had died of a broken heart, but his wife and brother Philip believed that he had been poisoned.

Philip had never liked the settlers, but from the day of his brother's death until the day of his own, he hated all white men and worked to be rid of them. "Only a small part of the land of my ancestors remains," he told a friend, "and I am determined not to live until I have no country."

Philip's first attack upon Plymouth Colony came in 1675, when some of his Indians fell upon the unsuspecting people of Swansea as they were leaving church. The attack on Swansea was followed in a few days by massacres at Dartmouth and Middleboro. "King" Philip's war had begun. Indians plundered and burned one village after another. No farm or house that stood alone was ever safe from their attack.

In the little village of Neponset, near Boston, there was one house that was almost as strong as a fort. To the Indians it looked like any ordinary large wooden house. But the English knew it had a secret. There was a house inside the house!

Beneath the weather-beaten wooden walls stood second walls of solid brick, so strong that they were bulletproof. Once the heavy doors were bolted and the shutters fastened, the people inside the Minot house would be safe.

One Sunday, in July, 1675, the two young children of John Minot were left in the house for a few hours, with one servant. The children played happily on the kitchen floor while the maid started food simmering in kettles over the fire. Then she pulled a chair toward the window.

"Come, little one," she said as she picked up

Suddenly the maid saw something that made her gasp

the baby, "let's watch for Mother and Father to come home."

Suddenly the maid saw something that made her gasp. An Indian, almost hidden behind a row of bushes in the garden, was creeping toward the house.

With the baby still on one arm, the girl sprang from her chair and ran to the door to slip the heavy bolts into place. She had no time to close the wooden shutters.

Oh, where can I hide the children? she thought, as she glanced around the kitchen. She saw no hiding place at all until she noticed, lying bottoms up on the floor, two huge brass kettles she had scoured the day before. Quickly she raised one kettle and shoved the baby under it; then before Little Brother knew what was happening—plop!—down came the second kettle over his head.

"Keep still, children," she warned as she ran upstairs to get John Minot's gun.

But the children did not keep still. They did not like being shoved under kettles and started to cry in anger. They tried to push the kettles over, but found them too heavy. This made them scream in terror, and the kettles rang with a wild, strange noise.

The Indian heard the dreadful racket as he approached the window, but he could see no one in the room. At that moment, the kettles started to crawl, moving slowly—slowly—slowly in his direction. He fired his gun at the strange, shining objects, but his shot did no harm.

The maid, who had by this time found John Minot's gun, took careful aim as she reached the kitchen door. She hit the Indian in the shoulder as he lowered his gun. He was crazed with pain and rage, and began to crawl through the kitchen window. Fighting bravely for her own life and the children's the girl then grabbed a shovelful of red-hot coals from the fireplace and tossed them in his face.

Only the burning, searing coals were able to make the Indian halt. Screaming with pain, he turned and ran into the woods. Later, he was found dead, several miles from the Minot house.

All the battles and raids of King Philip's War did not turn out so happily as this one for the settlers. Hundreds of colonists—men, women, and children—lost their lives. Others were kidnapped, tortured, or made slaves by the Indians. For awhile it looked as if the Indians would make good Philip's threat to drive the English out of New England.

Slowly, as time went on, the skirmishes and battles began to turn in the colonists' favor. A little over a year after the attack on the Minot house, Captain Benjamin Church, who was one of Plymouth's most daring Indian fighters, managed to corner Philip on a little knoll in a swamp near his home at Mount Hope. As Church and his forces closed in on their enemy, Philip tried desperately to escape, but was shot down by an Indian fighting on the side of the colonists. He fell on his face in the swamp mud—a bullet through his heart.

Chapter 17

OLD ANNAWON'S SURRENDER

AFTER PHILIP's death, only old Annawon, his greatest warrior, had the heart to fight on. It was his voice that was heard above the noise of battle shouting *"Iootash! Iootash!"* ("Stand firm! Stand firm!") to the Indians in the swamp who became panic-stricken after Philip had crumpled in the mud.

Old Annawon continued to prowl the countryside, killing the colonists and burning their homes wherever he stopped. The English thought him bold, cunning, and cruel, but to the Indians his was the only possible way to keep the land of their fathers.

Late in the summer of 1676, Captain Benjamin Church went after Annawon. He had a few men from Plymouth and a small group of friend-

ly Indians with him. They would be in great
danger, he knew, as Annawon was bent on re-
venging Philip's death.

Church's little "army" boldly advanced into
the territory between Mount Hope and Rehoboth where he heard the Indians had been
"rustling" cattle. It was not long before one of
his scouting parties found a few of Annawon's
men, who were foraging for food, and captured
them.

"Where is Annawon?" Church asked his
prisoners.

"We do not know. He moves the place where
he sleeps every night," they told him.

Church left most of his small force to guard
the prisoners and pushed on with only one man
from Plymouth and half a dozen Indian soldiers.
As they approached the place where he thought
his family was camped, one of the Indian soldiers
asked Church's permission to pay a visit to his
father.

"Where is he?" Church wanted to know.

"Only a few miles from here in the swamp," the Indian replied.

Church let him go, but followed at some distance with the rest of the men because there was always a chance that the Indian might lead him to Annawon. Church heard him shouting his father's name over and over as he moved deep into the swamp. Finally, they heard someone's answering call.

While waiting for his soldier to return, Church spied an almost hidden trail leading from the forest down into the swamp. He thought he heard someone approaching, and ordered his men to hide on both sides of the path. In a few minutes an old Indian with a gun on his shoulder appeared; behind him trudged a young squaw with a large basket.

Church and his soldiers leaped from their hiding places and captured the pair. Taking the girl to one side, Church questioned her, after first telling her what would happen if she lied to him.

"What person did you see last?"

"Captain Annawon."

"How many men does he have?"

"About fifty or sixty."

"How many miles away is he?"

"Miles? What are miles?" the girl asked, looking puzzled. "All I know is that he is in Squannaconk Swamp." This swamp lay between Rehoboth and Taunton.

Church could not be sure the girl was telling the truth. So he turned to the old man, who told him that he had been a member of Philip's war council. The old man gave much the same answers as the girl had given.

"Can we reach Squannaconk Swamp by the time it is dark?" Church asked the old Indian.

"If we start now and travel fast."

Something made Captain Church suddenly suspicious. "Who are you and why are you wandering around?" he snapped at his two prisoners, hoping to catch them off guard.

"I am one of Annawon's men. He has sent me to find out why the hunting party he sent out has not returned," was the Indian's frank reply.

As soon as the Indian, who had been looking for his father, returned, Church turned to his small force and asked, "How would you like to pay a surprise visit on Annawon?"

The men tried to tell him that it was not safe; now that Philip was dead, Annawon was the boldest, most dangerous Indian alive.

"I have hunted too long and too far for old Annawon to give up now, even if it costs me my life," said Church. He turned suddenly to the old man whom he had just captured. "Will you lead us to Annawon?"

"I have no choice, for you have spared my life," the Indian replied.

The party set off through the woods, swamp, and thickets at such a pace Captain Church could hardly keep the old man in sight. Just as the sun was setting, he came to a sudden stop.

"What is wrong?" asked Church.

"Nothing. Every day about this time Annawon sends out scouts. We must rest here until they go back to him."

When it began to grow dark, the old Indian stood up.

"Will you fight on our side?" Church asked, hoping that he would join the English force.

"Do not ask me to take arms against my old friend," the captive Indian begged. "I will go along with you and be helpful to you and will lay hand on any man who tries to hurt you— because you spared my life. But fight against Annawon—no."

After they had gone a short distance, they heard a sound. A soft thud-thud-thud—the sound of a woman pounding corn—told them they were approaching a camp.

Church and two of his Indians crept slowly, silently up a rocky cliff and looked down on the other side. Below them, they saw three companies of Indians camped at a little distance from each other, their bodies outlined by the light of their fires.

Church noticed that the warriors close to Annawon had stacked their guns for the night and covered them to protect them from the dampness. *Do I dare risk an attack?* he thought. *I have only a handful to their fifty or sixty. Perhaps I can win by a trick, but if it should fail* . . . He shuddered to think what would happen then.

Captain Church crept back to the old Indian. "How do we get down there?"

"Everyone has to come down the face of this cliff," the Indian whispered. "To come from any other direction is to risk being shot."

Church decided they would try to sneak down the cliff in the shadow of the old Indian and the girl. It was a daring plan and a dangerous one—so daring and so dangerous that no one would dream it would be tried! At some places the cliff was so steep they were forced to cling to saplings and bushes that sprouted from cracks in the ledge.

Thud-thud-thud. Thud-thud-thud. The welcome sound of the corn being pounded in the mortar covered the noise of their descent. When the squaw stopped to rest, they stopped, too. As soon as she took up her work again, Church and his party again dared to move.

So silently did they approach the camp that the unsuspecting Indians never guessed that an enemy was within six feet of them.

Suddenly, with a mighty leap, Church and his band jumped into the camp and made a grab for the guns that had been so carefully stacked.

Old Annawon started up with a hoarse cry of surprise. Church warned him that his camp was surrounded and there was no escape. The Indian soldiers with Church ran among Annawon's men telling them the same story. Convinced that Church had a large army ringing their camp, instead of the handful of men he actually had, old Annawon surrendered.

So far, so good, thought Church. *But from now on I must act every minute as though I really do have the army I claim to have.*

Putting on a brave front, Church turned to Annawon and asked, "What do you have for supper tonight? For I am come to sup with you."

"*Taubut*," replied the old chief, and called to his squaws to get some supper ready for the captain and his men. "What would you like, cow-beef or horse-beef?"

"Cow-beef," said Church without a moment's hesitation.

Supper was soon ready. Church pulled a little bag of salt out of his pocket—the only thing he had in the way of provisions! Carefully he salted his meat and the dried green corn the old squaw had been pounding. *How lucky for us that she was pounding corn in the mortar as we crept down,* he thought. *Otherwise, we would never have gotten here alive.*

After supper Church ordered several of his force to keep watch, and then he lay down to sleep. Old Annawon lay nearby. Church and Annawon tossed and turned; neither one was able to sleep. After a little while the old Indian got up and silently slipped away in the dark. He was gone so long that Church began to suspect trouble.

But Annawon finally came back, with a deer-

Kneeling beside Captain Church, he opened the bundle and spread out all the treasures

skin bundle in his arms. Kneeling beside Captain Church, he opened the bundle and spread out all the treasures of the Wampanoag nation.

There was a broad sachem belt edged with red hair that told, in designs worked in black and white wampum, the history of the tribes of the Wampanoag Federation. There was a smaller beaded band trimmed with red hair that Philip had worn on his head. There was a still smaller band with a star upon one end, that Philip had worn on his breast on state occasions.

Lifting a red blanket and two powder horns from the heap, Annawon held them up for Church to see. In a voice he could hardly keep steady, the old warrior said, "These are all that remain to us of our sachem, Pometacom."

After a minute, old Annawon continued in a voice choked with feeling, "Great Captain, you have killed Pometacom, the one whom you call 'Philip.' You have taken his lands, his fields, and hunting grounds. You have taken all else from us; take these, too."

Captain Church felt pity for Annawon. The

old Indian was his enemy and had brutally killed many colonists, but he was loyal and brave and true to his own people. Church gazed at the worn red blanket, the powder horns, and the beaded histories and thought, *These treasures mean to the Indians what the crown, robes, and sceptre of the King of England mean to us.*

The night slowly wore on.

Give me nerves of steel, the tired captain prayed. *If I make but a single slip so that the Indians suspect this camp is not ringed by an army, we shall still be slain.*

Captain Church, weary as he was, was able to keep his voice steady as he talked the rest of the night with Annawon. When dawn brightened the sky to the east, he rose, and gave orders to his men and their captives to march.

Chapter 18

1691

OLD ANNAWON's surrender brought the Wampanoag nation to an end. A few of Philip's people—those who refused to meet their harsh fate at the hands of the colonists—fled to the north and northwest. In later years, during the wars with the French and the Indians, some of these refugees may have had a part in the raids that again brought death and destruction to New England villages.

During King Philip's War, almost every Plymouth family lost someone dear to it. Many lost everything they had: relatives, homes, livestock, crops.

Plymouth itself did not live long as a separate colony after King Philip's War. Both New York and the Massachusetts Bay Colony were watching it with greedy eyes. Both wanted to annex it. In October, 1691, Massachusetts received a new royal charter and the "Old Colony" of Plymouth was included. By this time, John Cooke and Mary Allerton Cushman were the only ones left of the little band that had come in the *Mayflower* in 1620.

Only about fifty *Mayflower* Pilgrims had survived the first dreadful winter in the New World. From such a tiny start, the colony grew slowly. At the time King Philip's War broke out, more than half a century later, there were still less than seven thousand people in Plymouth Colony. It is the spirit of the little band, rather than its size, that has made the Pilgrims remembered.

"As one small candle may light a thousand," wrote Governor Bradford in 1630, "so the light here kindled hath shone unto many."

BOOKS ABOUT THE PILGRIMS
AND THEIR NEIGHBORS

Most books about the Pilgrims draw their information on the first two or three years in America from the same sources:

> Mourt, G.: *A relation, or journal of the beginnings and proceedings of the English plantation settled at Plimoth in New England.* London, 1622.

> Winslow, Edward: *Good Newes from New England.* London, 1624.

> Bradford, William: *Of Plimoth Plantation* 1620–1647. (Handwritten manuscript begun in 1630)

There was no such person as "G. Mourt." This name is believed to be a printer's error, for much of the book was written by William Bradford and Edward Winslow during the first year in America. Some of the manuscript was sent to England in the *Fortune* and was among the papers the pirates did not steal.

Good Newes from New England was written by Edward Winslow between 1621 and 1623. He took it to England with him in the fall of 1623 and it was this manuscript that Winslow worked over—polishing, changing a word here and there—as he whiled away the days aboard the *Anne*.

Both *Mourt's Relation,* as it is commonly known, and *Good Newes from New England* today would be called "on-the-spot" reporting of events in the New World and brought to the people back home in England the same kind of newsy information that a twentieth-century "space explorer" might write to friends back on earth.

Bradford's *Of Plimoth Plantation* was a different kind of "book." It was a history of the colony begun ten years after the Pilgrims first arrived in the New World. Bradford wrote in a vellum-covered notebook and worked on his history for twenty years. Because the writing took place so long after events occurred, Bradford omitted most of the little day-by-day happenings that made the other books so informative.

There is a mystery connected with the Bradford manuscript. During the American Revolution it disappeared from a library in Boston; nobody knew what had become of it. People thought the British must have destroyed it or that someone who knew its value had taken it as a souvenir.

More than fifty years passed. Then, in 1844, a book was published in England that quoted from the missing Bradford manuscript and told in a footnote that it was in the Fulham Palace Library of the Bishop of London.

One day, twelve years later, someone browsing in a Boston bookstore happened to pick up a copy of the imported English book. He read the footnote and realized its significance. The long-lost and priceless Bradford manuscript was still in existence!

Patriotic Americans got in touch with English authorities at once. The footnote was correct; the manuscript was in the Bishop of London's library, but neither the Bishop nor anyone else seemed to know where it had come from or when. Worst of all, the British government refused to give it up.

Many years were to pass before the British could be persuaded to part with the Bradford manuscript. When finally it was handed back to the United States in 1897, it had to come officially as the *Log of the Mayflower*. As a "history" of Plymouth Colony the British authorities would never give it up for it would be a state paper. But as a simple "log" of a ship—even though everyone knew that a "log" is not written ten years after the voyage—the manuscript could legally be returned.

Today many editions of Bradford's journal are available. The two most often consulted in the preparation of this book are:

> Bradford, William: *Bradford's History "of Plimoth Plantation,"* from the original manuscript with a report of the proceedings incident to the return of the manuscript to Massachusetts. Commonwealth of Massachusetts, 1898.

Bradford, William: *Of Plimoth Plantation* 1620–1647; a new edition: the complete text, with notes and an introduction by Samuel Eliot Morison. Knopf, 1952.

Most boys and girls will find these adult editions of Bradford too difficult. However, there are two books for young people, based in part on Bradford's history, that are only slightly harder to read than *Pilgrim Neighbors*. They are:

Morison, S. E. *The Story of the "Old Colony" of New Plymouth.* Knopf, 1956. (Covers years 1620–1692)

Smith, E. B. and Meredith, Robert, editors. *Pilgrim Courage*. Little Brown, 1962. (Covers years 1607–1621)

Excellent information on the early years of the Massachusetts Bay Colony is found in:

Higginson, Francis. *New England's Plantation.* London, 1630.

Winthrop, John. *History of New England* from 1630 to 1649.

A number of Winthrop editions are available; the one the author consulted was printed in Boston by Phelps and Farnham in 1825 and today is in the Rare Book Room of the Boston Public Library. On a flyleaf appear these words:

Given to the Prince Library of the Old South Society of Boston, Massachusetts by Nathaniel B. Shurtleff, M.D. in exchange for the "Bay State Psalms." January 11, 1860.

A story about the book in which this inscription appears is almost as strange as the one about the missing Bradford manuscript. Dr. Nathaniel B. Shurtleff, in 1860, persuaded one of the deacons of the Old South Church to trade the only perfect copy of the church library's three remaining *Bay Psalm Books* for two books that he owned.

The deacon did not know that a perfect copy of the *Bay Psalm Book* would soon become an almost priceless treasure. And to one who was not aware of the value of the books, an exchange of two for one looked like a good bargain. Today, the 1825 edition of the Winthrop history that the library received in the "swap" has little value, but the psalm book that Dr. Shurtleff managed to get might easily bring over $200,000 in the rare book market.

Governor John Winthrop of Massachusetts Bay Colony kept a journal of everything important that occurred from the time he first embarked in England in 1630 until the year 1644. Although he may have intended his diary for publication, it remained in the Winthrop family in manuscript form. About the time of the American Revolution, Governor Trumbull of Connecticut borrowed it from Winthrop's heirs and copied part of it with the help of his secretary, John Porter. The copy that Shurtleff exchanged, in his famous "swap," had been printed from the manuscript originally made by Trumbull and Porter and rechecked by Porter in 1788 to clear up any errors they might have made earlier.

One of the most readable of all early sources consulted was the "entertaining history," as it was called, of King Philip's War. Based on the notes and documents hoarded through the years by the most daring of all seventeenth-century Indian fighters, it is as interesting a story today as it was in 1716.

> Church, Thomas. *The Entertaining History of King Philip's War* . . . as told by Colonel Benjamin Church to his son . . . Boston 1716.

Captain Benjamin Church was a very old man in 1716, so he had his son do the actual writing. This explains why the book is written in the third person. The author worked from a copy of the second edition, "reprinted and sold" in 1772 by Solomon Southwick of Newport, Rhode Island.

The 1772 edition is famous for a frontispiece signed by Paul Revere. The pop-eyed, baby-faced man in this portrait does not look at all the way one would expect a daring Indian fighter to look.

Again, we are up against a mystery. This portrait is not a picture of Church. For some unknown reason a print of Charles Churchill, English poet, had been "converted" into Benjamin Church, Indian fighter, simply by hanging a powder horn around the poet's neck!

Very little for children has been written on King Philip's War. However, for adults there is a book that interprets that conflict as we would today view a clash between developed and underdeveloped peoples. Parents or teachers, whose interest in King Philip's War has been whetted by reading with children chapters 16 and 17 of *Pilgrim Neighbors,* will be able to get an adult's view of the conflict in:

> Leach, Douglas Edward. *Flintlock and Toma-hawk; New England in King Philip's War.* Macmillan, 1958.

INDEX

167